TOUGH CHOICES & HARD DECISIONS

Rebuilding India
The Next 25 Years

New India Post COVID

Rajendra Pratap Gupta

INDIA · SINGAPORE · MALAYSIA

Notion Press

Old No. 38, New No. 6
McNichols Road, Chetpet
Chennai - 600 031

First Published by Notion Press 2020
Copyright © Rajendra Pratap Gupta 2020
All Rights Reserved.

ISBN

Hardcase: 978-1-64899-609-2
Paperback: 978-1-64892-975-5

Only once before, we had a chance to build a ravaged nation after the British left India in 1947, and now again in 2020, due to the COVID-19, we have another opportunity to Rebuild India.

We got freedom in 1947 and now, we need to be self-reliant.

Time to rebuild New India is 'NOW'!

Disclaimer

- All the charts, diagrams, and data are sourced, and their references are given.

- Data are only for indicative and representation purposes.

- Weblinks given are functional at the time of writing.

- I have made every effort to ensure that due credit is given through proper citations of quotes, articles, and other texts referenced and images used. While expressing any factual instance or data, I have done my best to rely on credible and documented sources. Yet, there is a possibility of a human error. Also, given the importance of timing for this book on Rebuilding Indian Economy in light of COVID-19, this book was completed in nine days, and so, it will have 'misses' and 'mistakes' both.

- My knowledge is limited to the documents and reports available in the public domain on the statistics and programs. I could have got deeper into suggesting more or perhaps better solutions for every sector if there was a 'Knowledge Paper' on the 'State of Economy' due to COVID-19. However, with whatever is available, I have tried to do my best in the nine days of writing this book.

- In case you find any error or discrepancy, please contact me, and I will ensure that the same are addressed in the subsequent edition of the book.

- Trade names/marks used may belong to third parties and have been quoted just for the sake of information to the audience.

- Statements in italics are original quotes coined for this book, unless followed by a reference. They should be attributed to the author, if quoted.

- Please do not copy or reproduce in whole or part thereof, the contents of this book without the written permission from the author.

I dedicate this book to

India's Future   —   Youth

Wealth Creators   —   Farmers, Small Traders and Shopkeepers, and Solo Entrepreneurs

Soldiers   —   Troops at the borders, Teachers, Frontline Health Workers who secure India

Unsung Heroes   —   Who keep India going, and most importantly – Unorganised Workers & CSOs

Senior citizens   —   Whom we need to look after

Left behind   —   Whom we missed taking along in our journey

Dr. Mohan Bhagwat, for his inspiration and encouragement.

Dr. Murli Manohar Joshi, for bringing me into the realm of policy-making and guiding me.

Shri. Narendra Modi for being our Prime Minister, with whom ideas can be expected to be implemented quickly. I took to writing this book on 19th April and completed it on 28th April, knowing for sure, that he is open to new ideas and converts ideas into programs for implementation. His leadership is assuring enough that we will be out of the woods and will emerge stronger than ever before.

Shri. Amit Shah who believes only in data and facts, and I am sure this book has it in plenty.

Shri. J.P. Nadda, for his guidance, handholding and supporting me during my working with the Government, and for his message, 'Policy is about giving a direction.'

My mother, Dr. Sarojini Devi Gupta, who fought stage IV cancer, and on 28th April in 1997, left us to serve the almighty. Her dedication, truthfulness, commitment, and helping nature continues to guide me, as I complete this book on her 23rd death anniversary.

Contents

Other Books by the Author

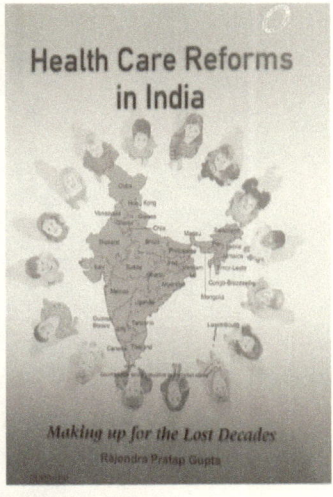

About the Author

Prof. Rajendra Pratap Gupta is a sought-after policymaker, who has contributed to policymaking across governance, health, education, and economy. He has been contributing to policy making for over a decade not just in India, but also globally, working with various governments, government agencies, different multi-lateral bodies, and with global organizations.

Rajendra had one of the fastest rises in the corporate world and became the Chief Operating Officer in the 8th year and Chief Executive Officer in the 9th year of starting his career. He has served at senior-most levels at fortune 20 & fortune 500 companies in India and advised organizations across; USA, Europe, U.K., Middle East, and India. He has been invited by global organizations like the United Nations, UNESCO, World Bank, Asian Development Bank, World Health Organization, World Economic Forum, and International Telecommunications Union. Also by the United States of America, Governments of Japan, Finland, Algeria & Bangladesh, and also by the Ministry of Health, Ministry of Human Resource Development, Ministry of Labour and Employment & The Planning Commission – Government of India, for his views on a diverse range of issues.

He played a significant role in drafting public policies and became the youngest person to draft the election manifesto of BJP at the age of 37 in 2009. He also played a significant role in drafting the BJP's Lok Sabha Election Manifesto in 2014. Besides, he has played an important role in preparing the National Health Policy 2017, National Education Policy, the policy (schemes) for Building & Other Construction Workers (BOCW) – Ministry of Labour & Employment, Government of India, & the State Health Policy for Uttar Pradesh. He is currently drafting the national guidelines for Digital Health. He is a serial social entrepreneur and has founded several social impact organizations; HIMSS India, Disease Management Association of India (An organization with a special consultative status with the United Nations ECOSOC), Continua India, PCHA India, 'Government Industry Dialogue' Initiative, and the Centre for Participatory Democracy.

In 2012, he was felicitated by the sheriff of Los Angeles, named the 'Thought Leader of the Year' three years in a row, and featured amongst the '25 Living Legends of Healthcare in India'. In 2012, he was nominated to World Economic Forum's Global Agenda Council, and he still serves on the World Economic Forum's Expert Network. He has authored three best-selling books:

1. Healthcare Reforms in India – Making up for the lost decades. This book led to significant healthcare reforms in India, and the National Health Policy incorporated many suggestions mentioned in this book, including the 'Pre-emptive care model.'

2. Your Vote is Not Enough – This book highlights the role of citizens in policy formulation and how ordinary citizens can drive changes in policy. Key ideas presented in this path-breaking book are under implementation.

3. Your Degree is Not Enough – Education for GenNext. This book is about transforming the education system with practical and innovative ideas and prepare the students for the future.

Rajendra has served as an advisor to the Union Minister for Health & Family Welfare, Government of India. Also, he has served as a member of the National Education Policy Committee, Ministry of Human Resource Development, Government of India, a member of the Khadi & Village Industries Commission, Government of India, and has served on various committees of the Government.

He holds a Bachelor's degree in science and social science, and a Master's degree in Innovation & Change Management from the York St. John University, U.K. Besides, he has done the executive education program from the Harvard Business School & Kellogg School of Business, USA. He has served as a 'Distinguished Professor of Innovation' at a Central Government University, and was conferred Honorary Professorship at Amity University, and Gulf Medical University, UAE.

Rajendra travels extensively and has delivered over 200 talks across the world on a range of topics.

Connect with the Author

 https://www.facebook.com/rajendragupta

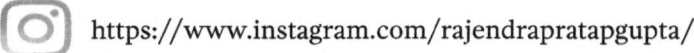 https://www.linkedin.com/in/rajendragupta/

 https://www.instagram.com/rajendrapratapgupta/

 https://twitter.com/RajendraGupta

rajendrapratapgupta@yahoo.com

About the Book

In fact, after writing three books on healthcare, public policy, and education, I had started work on a book on how to make India a developed country titled, 'The Next Twenty Five Years', and it is a one year project to be completed in 2021. I am still working on the book but, due to COVID-19, I decided to come out with this book on the plan of action (programs) needed immediately due to the ravaging impact of COVID-19 on the Indian economy and society. We know for a fact that incremental changes will not be enough to resurrect the economy, as our demographic dividend will only last for another 25 years. So we have only 25 years, in which we have to make careful short-term and long-term choices, build new institutions, and start new programs to build a nation of happy and progressive citizens.

If we handle the COVID-19 crisis with a long-term vision, India can come out of the Lower-Middle Income Country (LMIC) status in the next five years and become a developed country in the next 20 years. This book is about making India stronger, self-sufficient, and a developed country in the next quarter of the century.

We were all waiting for the year 2020 with great excitement for many years because it is no ordinary year- it is the start of the new decade, and we have read many books envisioning India of 2020. The new year started on a sombre note with Australian bush fires and fires in Amazon, which threatened our ecology and, reeling from an environmental threat, we entered 2020 – only to be hit by 'COVID-19' (Corona Virus Disease 2019). It started from Wuhan and, within a quarter, has brought the entire world to a grinding halt. Never before in human history we have witnessed such a situation. COVID-19 has impacted every single human being on this planet.

Developing economies are hit the hardest with low incomes, low spending, and now, with the economy in a standstill, we face tough times ahead. For us, post-COVID-19, our strengths will become our weaknesses, and we should be prepared to address the same. Given the current experience, major economies will reset their supply chains, and we will no longer be suppliers of HCQ (Hydroxychloroquine) to the world, and similarly, many other things will change. Also, we should not be dependent for APIs on China. So, this is the best time to bring in radical changes (transformation) and go back to the drawing board. We need to rebuild India.

Only one Prime Minister earlier had this opportunity in the history of India, Pandit Jawaharlal Nehru. When he started (after India securing Independence from the British Rule), Nehru had the complete freedom to lay the future of the nation – with no opposition to whatever he wanted to do. Everyone wanted a new India after centuries of the fight to oust the British. Now, Shri Narendra Modi has a similar opportunity but with many more advantages. We are financially stable as a nation today with a healthier population (and a much bigger population too). Technologically, we are much more advanced with some good educational institutions in every field.

Moreover, India is amongst the top economies in the world with decent foreign reserves. The best part, Narendra Modi, in a real sense, has no opposition, and more importantly, is backed by the formidable ground force of the RSS. The trust factor in Narendra Modi from the general masses is extraordinary, and this is another reason and a wonderful opportunity to build a 'New India.'

In this historic transformation, it will need continuous engagement and action by an aware citizen like you. India's journey cannot start with you being a silent spectator or a passive contributor. You have to play the role of an active contributor and beneficiary of India's most crucial march to getting out of the LMIC (Lower Middle-Income Country) status within the next five years, and also, becoming a developed country over the next quarter of a century.

It all depends on the steps you take and how you partner and benefit from this journey. You, a citizen (whether you are a professional, bureaucrat, politicians or self-employed) of this great country, will have to take a call on which project you would like to work – if you would like to be an entrepreneur, or associate with a project or a program, or volunteer in your free time, and only then, it will help in achieving our national goal of becoming a developed nation with happy citizens. It is a lifetime opportunity, and these are tough goals, and it will mean a big thing to transform this mega democracy, but is it doable? The answer is short, 'Together, we can'.

So, let's make it happen and take the first step!

The Current Situation

It's a New Dawn for a New World!

Never before this, humanity has faced such a lockdown ever. COVID-19 started as an epidemic (a widespread occurrence of an infectious disease in a community at a particular time), and within a few weeks, this had become a pandemic (prevalent over a whole country or the world). Today, we can call it an 'Apocalypsedemic' (apocalypse – the complete final destruction of the world, as described in the biblical book of Revelation) for businesses and daily wagers. It has deprived millions of their livelihoods and for some, even lives, and as I write, the global incidence is about 3.2 million with more than 228,000 deaths across 190 countries, and counting!

COVID-19 indeed has challenged science, systems, and strategy. India, being a country aspiring to be a 5 trillion dollar economy by 2025, needs to go back to the drawing board to start again. On one side, we need stimulus, but most importantly, we need a new system!

Millions of migrants – daily wage workers, would have either migrated or should be in the process of migration back to their native places, and given their experience due to COVID-19, some may not return. So, it will have its long term impact on the working population shifts, and also on the business environment, in the immediate, medium, and long-term.

Also, we keep saying, anything we do for 21 days becomes a habit. Most of the people have crossed twenty-one days in isolation (lockdown), and so they have, for sure, given up some old habits or picked up new habits, and thus, it will be a change of life and lifestyle when the world opens again. The world will become more transactional than ever before.

The world can never be the same again!

Global Forecasts and India

'COVID-19 started as a local infection in a global manufacturing city, and soon turned into a global pandemic resulting in a logistics issue, and this having prolonged for weeks, led to a human resource issue and a cash flow issue, and finally, it will a demand issue, and will end into an economic issue, pulling down the global economies'.

Though it is too early to make a forecast, but some multi-lateral bodies, rating agencies, even banks, have jumped the gun and made predictions, but well, that's their job! Most of the stock markets and also the financial markets make the best out of speculation and long-term forecasts.

According to the World Trade Organization (WTO), global trade is likely to fall between 13 to 32% in 2020 (WTO, 2020), and every region will suffer a double-digit decline. According to the World Bank (Maliszewska, Mattoo, & Mensbrugghe, 2020), the global GDP is likely to fall between 2.1–3.9%. According to the International Monetary Fund (IMF), global growth will fall below -7.4% (Adrian & Natalucci, 2020), and according to the Chief Economist of IMF, the projected global growth in 2020 is likely to fall to -3% (Gopinath, 2020).

According to the Organization for Economic Co-operation and Development (OECD), for every month of lockdown, there will be a loss of 2 percentage points in annual GDP growth (OECD, 2020). According to the International Labour Organization (ILO), COVID is going to impact 2.7 billion workers, representing about 81% of the global workforce. Businesses are facing catastrophic losses, and as on 1st April 2020, ILO expects that it will have an impact equivalent to laying off of 195 million full-time workers in the current quarter, and the final tally for 2020 could be far more. Sectors that employ about 1.25 billion workers, representing 38% of the global workforce, are at risk due to severe decline and will face the risk of workforce displacement, particularly in Low and Middle-Income Countries. About 2 billion workers are in informal employment, and most of them are in emerging and developing countries, which will be under financial distress due to the impact of COVID. For India, where 90% work in the informal economy, about 400 million workers are vulnerable and are likely to slide into poverty (ILO, 2020). It is a known fact that pay-cuts and employees being 'furloughed' or sent on 'leave without pay', will lead to increase in the population of the 'working poor' (working poor are the people who are working or in jobs, but their incomes fall below the poverty line).

Barclay's, an investment bank's forecast about India's economic growth is startling, as it predicts that India's economic growth will fall to Zero. (Mishra A.R., 2020). Though I believe that India, being an agriculture-based economy, will not be impacted to an extent that the growth falls to zero. If we look at the numbers of this sector, the gross value added (GVA) by agriculture, forestry and fishing to the economy is about INR 18.55 lakh crore (Financial year-2019), and about 58 percent of the population still is dependent on agriculture as its primary source of livelihood (IBEF, 2020). Agriculture and its allied sectors, despite COVID-19, have not been impacted much, and so, talking of 'Zero' percent growth makes such a forecast seems *implausible and far-fetched*.

A few things don't require assumptions given the reality on ground, the sentiment emerging from the grim scenario, and the uncertainty around the progression of COVID-19. Some indicators are emerging and pointing towards a need for action:

- COVID-19 has proven that countries with higher GDP are not super-powers. They have suffered equally, if not more, and failed to contain the impact of the virus. So, even as a developing country, we have a better scope for planned progress, so that we don't have to give up before an invisible enemy as we continue to march on our economic development.

- COVID-19 will lead to a resetting of the global supply chains, leading to self-sufficient and inward-looking economies the world over – its the death of Globalization (at least for essential supplies) which the US propagated a few decades ago. Also, this being the election year in the USA, it will fast-track protectionism. India has to respond to make the best out of the emerging opportunity immediately.

- COVID-19 has led to unmasking and unearthing redundancies in the corporate world, and we will be a more lean and agile world, going forward. One critical fallout will be mass scale adoption of automation. Indiscriminate Automation can lead to socio-economic unrest. India must find a middle path for cautiously adopting technology.

- Given that large segments of populations in Lower and Middle-Income Countries are migrant workers, even if the COVID recedes by June, workers are not going to return immediately to cities to work in factories. In fact, given their experience and uncertainty during these times, a section of the workers may stay back with their families in their native places. Even, according to the Transporter's Association, there has been the incidence of truckers abandoning stranded vehicles (TNN, 2020), which means, that these truck drivers also are not going to return back soon.

So, manufacturing, construction, transport, logistics, tourism, restaurants, and small entrepreneurs will suffer a significant jolt, and it is not going to return to normal in the next few quarters. What steps could neutralize the impact and prop up these sectors?

- Though the government is offering financial help, the forbearance limit of about 600 million-plus people will be put to the test over the next few months, and we should be ready for the mass outburst of anger and violence. It is a real threat, not to be taken lightly. So, how can the state governments prepare to handle the emerging scenario?

- Majority of the businesses, due to competition, work on a wafer-thin margin and operate on a sub-ten percent margin. Being closed for about two months means going out of business.

- Individual suppliers of services will be the worst hit. Will the financial package (stimulus) be enough? What is needed to bring them back as engines for growth?

- COVID-19 has put the disaster management system and the healthcare system to the ultimate test. What will happen when the lockdown is lifted? Imagine AIIMS or similar public institutions at the district and state level where the OPD (Out-patient department) registration numbers are in thousands for secondary care or tertiary care patients – daily! How will these institutions handle the workload, and what will happen to the elective surgeries postponed? Will this mean a new start for digital health? A new way to report and manage epidemics through digital tools? Can this change the healthcare delivery altogether, and will healthcare be able to embrace the new paradigm immediately, and what are the preparations needed for the same?

- Agriculture remains the insurance for the flattening economy, but the question is, can it keep the urban economy afloat for long? Will MSP (Minimum Support Price) be enough to boost the profitability of agriculture? Is increasing agriculture profitability enough, or we need to go beyond ?

- A new paradigm of virtual or digital offices has emerged, which is not just cost-friendly – but also eco-friendly. How can entrepreneurs leverage this opportunity, and in which sectors will entrepreneurial opportunities arise, and how can the government support the entrepreneurship ecosystem?

- Can India emerge as the new hardware and software superpower? What do we need to do?

- While we put NPAs (Non-Performing Assets) in abeyance, what can we do to avoid the next NPA bubble?

Also, as one looks at the emerging scenario, and this is when COVID-19 is still reigning terror, we need to consider some other facts as mentioned below:

- When will the global economy be back on its feet? It is tough to analyse as there is no precedent of such a lockdown ever! *But for sure, essential goods will face a 20–25 percent decline in demand and non-essential goods will see a much steeper decline.*

- If we look at the SME sector, a recent survey reveals that nearly half (47%) of the small businesses have either run out of cash or are close to it, due to the market slowdown and closure.

- Twenty-four percent of the SMEs had cash reserves to last them for 1–3 months, while twenty-three percent can sustain between 3–6 months and six percent can last six months at the current rate of cash burn, and thirteen percent of the SMEs were considering to shut down their business (The Banking & Finance Post, 2020).

- According to a study by All India Manufacturer's Organization (AIMO), about 25 percent of the more than 7.5 crore MSMEs in India will face closure if the lockdown is for four weeks, and about 43 percent will face closure if the lockdown extends to over eight weeks, and this will impact 11.4 crore people employed with MSMEs, which contribute about 30–35 percent to the GDP (KPMG, 2020, p. 47).

- Even essential services like hospitals (which actually should be in demand due to this pandemic), are in dire straits. Hospitals have been severely impacted and are under huge losses as the occupancy has plummeted from a high of 90–95 percent to a low of 20 percent since the beginning of COVID-19, resulting to a 65–80 percent dip in their revenues. They don't expect to return to normal in the next 4–6 months (Didyala, 2020).

- According to Boeing, the world's leading plane manufacturer, it may take two to three years to be back to normal (Tangel, 2020), and a similar situation prevails in other sectors as well. All this is going to have a cascading effect for which the policymakers need to be prepared. It is not the time for business as usual, and it calls for designing a new system.

- According to Harvard Business Review (Tarki, Levy, & Weiss, 2020), *'During the crisis, the path between corporate denials and layoffs is often a short one. For weeks, our corporate clients and contacts waved off concerns about a potential economic impact from the COVID-19 outbreak. Then something changed around 9th March.*

First, our contacts told us they were restricting visitors to their offices and encouraging remote work. Now, only a few weeks later, we are hearing that many of them are considering layoffs to ensure they make it through the crisis – and a recent survey found that a vast majority of corporate leaders are considering some sort of financial action as a result of the pandemic'. So, corporate India will not behave differently in such an extreme crisis. The economy will take a hit.

'Once the lockdown is over, supplies will resume, but demand will continue to be an issue for a few quarters, and this is where the government has a major role to play'.

Tough Choices & Hard Decisions

When we are in a tough situation, we are faced with tough choices and have to take hard decisions. Also, tough circumstances compel us to think under pressure, which means – thinking about newer possibilities and in an innovative manner.

But one rule of thumb is that, the more you delay in making hard decisions, the bigger the price you will pay. It is in the interest of the nation and its 1.35 billion population that hard decisions be taken to make India, a land of our dreams. We will build and benefit from it. COVID-19 is the right opportunity to work towards making India a developed country in the next quarter of a century, and make it self-reliant and prosperous. Some of the options for the tough choices, followed by hard decisions we need to make, are mentioned ahead.

Lobbying for Policy Making or Crowd Sourcing Policy Inputs

Modi led government is perhaps the first one, where efforts have been taken to involve the people in policy-making by crowdsourcing inputs and ideas through the Prime Minister's social media and government portals. Still, lobby houses masquerading as industry representative associations have an undue influence on policy briefings to the government and the resultant policy making. This has, for long, sabotaged any worthwhile policy formulation or evidence-based policymaking. Even in healthcare, which is considered as a social sector, almost half a dozen lobbying organizations have come up in the past decade, backed by common investors – big business houses, to twist the policies to favour them. While it creates an impression that multiple industry organizations are demanding similar relief/policy reform from the government, it is actually that the same investors are behind all such organizations most of the time, and this creates a misconception on the need for a particular reform.

I write this with the first-hand experience as a policymaker. Let me give you an example of how these lobbying organizations have little to do with the national interest, except to ensure favourable policy framework for their members – large corporate houses! When I was drafting the Election Manifesto of the BJP in 2014, none of the industry bodies had answers to my three queries;

1. How do I reduce the country's import bill and strengthen the rupee through manufacturing semi-conductor chips and electronics in India, bills for which would cross our oil import bill in the next two decades

2. Innovation in different sectors and,

3. Job creation and Value addition to farming.

They took a good 6–8 weeks to come back with the information, which should ideally have been a part of their initial inputs considering the national interest.

So, we have to make a **hard decision** to choose between these lobbying organizations and crowdsourcing policy inputs.

Small Number of Large Companies or Large Number of Small Companies

The country has to decide – whether we want to follow the current model of having a small number of large companies or move to a model that has a large number of small companies. For a country like India with 640 districts (CENSUS 2011, n.d.), according to the Oxfam report (OXFAM International, 2020);

- 1% of the top 10% Indian population holds 77% of the total national wealth. 73% of the wealth generated in 2017 went to the wealthiest 1% while the 67 crore Indians who comprise the poorest half of the population saw only a 1% increase in their wealth.

- India produced 70 new millionaires every day.

- There are 119 billionaires in India, and the number of billionaires increased from 9 in 2000 to 101 in 2017.

- It would take 941 years for a minimum wage worker in rural India to earn what the top paid executive at a leading Indian garment company makes in a year.

While having wealthy people is neither bad nor wrong, but having a few wealthy families at the cost of the poor is not just bad for the society and economy, but also for the democracy. We all know that the wealthy (big corporate houses) have access to the politicians, decision-makers, and power-brokers, and they will keep twisting the rules to ensure that their wealth and prosperity are protected. India, historically, has been a nation of farmers and traders, and that is what created a society that maintained equilibrium. Also, if we consider the 'Cost of job creation' as mentioned ahead – the 'cost of job creation' in larger enterprises is much higher as compared to the 'cost of job creation' in smaller enterprises, which is a major argument in favour of shifting to smaller enterprises (MSMEs). We need to learn from the German Mittelstand. I wrote an article about this more than five years ago (Gupta R.P., Economy, 2015), and I am reproducing a small abstract from the article below.

German Mittelstand. Germany as a country has done well compared with others, and here comes an important lesson for India—German Mittelstand (SMEs in Germany). SMEs in Germany had the most significant contribution to high employment and productivity. Here are some interesting statistics, from the Federal Ministry of Economics and Technology, Germany:

- More than 99% of all German firms (3.7 million) belong to SMEs.

- SMEs contribute to almost 52% of the total economic output, totaling a turnover of Euro 2 trillion.

- SMEs employ 60% of employees, subject to social security contributions, and employ 83.2% of trainees.

- 95% of Germany's SMEs are family-owned.

- German SMEs are the most innovative in Europe and supply goods all over the world, and there are some 1,300 world market leaders from the German Mittelstand.

- They cover all sectors like electrical, engineering, and industrial products.

- SMEs are major contributors to low youth unemployment in Germany, as compared to other European nations.

- The 'Make it in Germany' website is a supporter of the initiative (Gupta R.P., Can Make In India Learn From Make It In Germany, 2015).

Now, we need to go back to the drawing board and redo our economic model, which should aim at self-sufficiency at the district level, and based on a large number of small enterprises. We need to create distinct economies based on local geography, climate, and demography.

We have to give up this metro-centric economic model and decentralize the growth model. The new economic model should create not only local vibrant communities and sustainable economies, but also de-risk our long-term growth by decentralizing it. I mention about the roadmap on how to achieve this 'Distributed Growth Model' in the chapters ahead.

So, the **hard decision** for India would be to move away from patronizing 'Small number of large companies to a large number of small enterprises'.

Making Agriculture Profitable or an Attractive Business

A lot of things have been tried to make agriculture profitable, but so far, it has not worked. Despite the M.S.Swaminathan committee in 2004, more than a decade and a half later, not much has changed, and farmer's suicides continue to rise (Express News Service, 2020). The MSP (Minimum Support Price) approach to profitability does not work because you get MSP only when you produce crops! I think, we need to go beyond MSP to make agriculture not just profitable, but also an attractive business or a profession. How will that happen? It requires a holistic plan, which I discuss in the chapter on the 'Distributed Growth Model'.

So, the **hard decision** is, to go beyond making agriculture profitable, and work towards making agriculture an attractive business!

Genetically Modified and Chemical Farming or Organic Farming

The world over, there is a definite shift towards organic and natural products, and it presents a global opportunity for Indian agriculture. The change is happening in the western world, and it will keep increasing with time. This fact is validated by the area under organic farming growing steadily (Thacker, 2020). Also that, the organic food market in the US surpassed US\$45 billion turnovers in 2017, a good six percent increase over 2016. Also, the area under organic farming has increased by twenty percent in the US, between 2011 and 2018 (Cernansky, 2018).

Indian agriculture will benefit immensely by focusing on nutritious crops, and also by moving solely towards organic farming, over the course of a decade. Besides, being environmentally friendly, it is also health-friendly, and is here to stay. Lastly, organic farming is native to India and of late, government has been pushing for 'Zero budget farming.' With India moving towards organic farming, the amount of money spent on the fertilizer subsidy, which is about to touch Rs. 80,000 crore (PTI, Agriculture, 2019), can be invested in research and development of organic farming, in promotion and marketing of organic produce, and making India the world leader in organic farming.

So, the **hard decision** is – making a switch to Non-Chemical, Non-GM – Organic farming.

Loan Waiver or Loan Deferment

Loan waivers have long been used during election season and have caused a loss of tens of thousands of crores, but the bigger question is, did it really address the issues which caused these loans to become a liability? The government must take steps to boost the income of farmers so that they can repay the loans taken. It looks like the loan waivers have become election year issues. It is time that the Government takes a decision that the loans will not be waived, but only deferred, or staggered payment will be allowed in case of natural calamities or crop damage, and when the loan deferment happens, the insurance cannot be claimed. This loan waiver is a political contagion and has now become a regular feature during election season across states. All political parties must agree that none of them will ask or support loan waivers, and the only relief that could be given is loan deferment, and interest waiver in exceptional circumstances.

This is one of the **hard decisions** to be made before it is too late; instead of waiver, there should only be a deferment.

Energy Generation or Renewable Energy & Conservation

A country that is aspiring to be an Upper-Middle Income Country in the next five years, and a developed country in the next quarter of a century, it will undoubtedly need the power to fuel its growth. Moreover, due to Digital Empowerment, we will need to be 'always connected'. The requirement for the massive energy needs of a country with 1.35 billion population calls for careful planning. It is projected that India will consume more power than the United States of America by 2045, mostly driven by air conditioners and electric vehicles (Dutta S., 2019). Due to increased demand, there is going to be a massive gap created between the demand and supply of electrical energy in the next twenty-five years (by 2045) in Business As Usual (BAU) scenario.

It is expected that, by 2045, the gap between India's energy needs and supply is likely to be 40% (Shodhganga, 2020, p. 37). Given the current production patterns, we are going to have another major issue of emission of greenhouse gases (GHG) due to dominating fossil fuel-based electricity production. Also, by 2045, the major electricity consumers will be industry – domestic, commercial, and others. The commercial sector will consume 26 percent, and the transport sector will also be growing at an average growth rate of 5.9%.

But, when it comes to energy savings and carbon dioxide reduction, the potential for energy conservation can be used to reduce the electricity demand by 40% in the year 2045, and this will also reduce the emission of GHGs (Shodhganga, 2020, p. 47).

Also, given the fact that India has one of the largest reserves of thorium, we must consider nuclear energy as a critical resource to meet our ever-increasing energy needs (IBEF, 2020, p. 10).

Given that India has been blessed with abundant sunlight throughout the year, we must massively invest in solar power and utilize nuclear power, besides wind power. Considering that the flow of rivers is not the same as it was three decades ago, we must show restraint in hydropower generation, except for high gradient rivers with perennial water flow.

So, the **hard decision** here is, between ramping up our energy generation as per the current production scenario, which leads to high GHGs, or using renewable sources of energy, nuclear power, and energy savings (conservation). The choice is a no brainer.

Divesting PSUs or Building SPSUs

When the nation achieved independence, the vision behind setting up PSUs was to build strategic assets for rapid industrialization from a predominantly agrarian economy, and create income and jobs. Later, the private banks were nationalized in 1969 and 1980. Now, the government is trying to divest the PSUs and even the profitable ones. Well, the thinking is that, the government's job is to regulate businesses and not run them, and also that, this divestment program is driven for two major reasons: First, the government is in desperate need of money due to fiscal deficit, and second, some PSUs like Air India are under heavy losses. One crucial point to ponder is that, when the private sector is handed over the same PSUs, it turns them profitable, but the successive governments have failed to turn them around and deliver profits. So, the issue is of professional management and not anything else. So, yes, the government should consider retaining and investing in building S-PSUs (PSUs with strategic importance) to the nation like in defence, hospitals, logistics, and pharmaceuticals (vaccines and API manufacturers), and for the rest, we can divest. We will need Strategic PSUs (SPSUs), which are run professionally and also on a 50:50 partnership, where the government invests, and the private sector runs it and delivers profit. The government should nominate sectoral experts on the board with clearly defined charter and deliverables, and no bureaucrat – serving or retired, should ever be appointed on the PSU boards. This is the only way for the government to build and own, but not operate these assets, except for defense, space, nuclear plants, etc. – which have strategic importance.

So, the **hard decision** is, instead of just divesting blindly, we must equally invest and build Strategic PSUs for national security.

Automation or Sustainable Automation

COVID-19 has led to unmasking and unearthing of redundancies in the corporate world, and moving forward, we will be a more lean and agile world. So, on one side, we will have pay cuts and retrenchment, and on the other side, we will be impacted by automation, and this is something we must address through a well-defined policy framework.

Given that large segments of populations in Lower and Middle-Income Countries are migrant workers, even if COVID recedes by May-June, workers are not going to return immediately to cities to work in factories and other establishments. In fact, given their experience and uncertainty during these times, a section of the workers may stay back with their families in their native places. So, manufacturing, construction, travel, and tourism, and small entrepreneurs will suffer a significant jolt, and the situation is not going to return to normal by Q3, 2020.

Another significant change that has happened is the 'work from home' culture. This will also free up a lot of office space and even lead to new job profiles, which are 'task-driven' and 'job-driven,' and may not require workers to work 5 or 6 days per week. So, some employees may be renegotiated to three or four days a week work profile. Besides these redundancies; business organizations, and manufacturing will resort to automation to become independent of future uncertainties due to COVID-19 like outbreaks, which means, they will resort to automation – from reception, assembling – to logistics i.e. front end to backend integration across the value chain. Indiscriminate adoption of automation is where the world faces significant, long-term societal risk. Estimates before COVID have quantified that automation could replace 40 percent of jobs (Reisinger, 2019) and post COVID-19, this is likely to increase. According to the World Bank (Chuah, Loayza, & Schmillen, 2018), *"Smart machines probably won't kill us all—but they'll take our jobs, and sooner than you think"*.

Post the COVID shutdown, automation will get fast-tracked. A few companies which wanted to lay off people but could not, will now use COVID as an excuse to lay off people.

Saving jobs is now a bigger challenge than creating jobs!

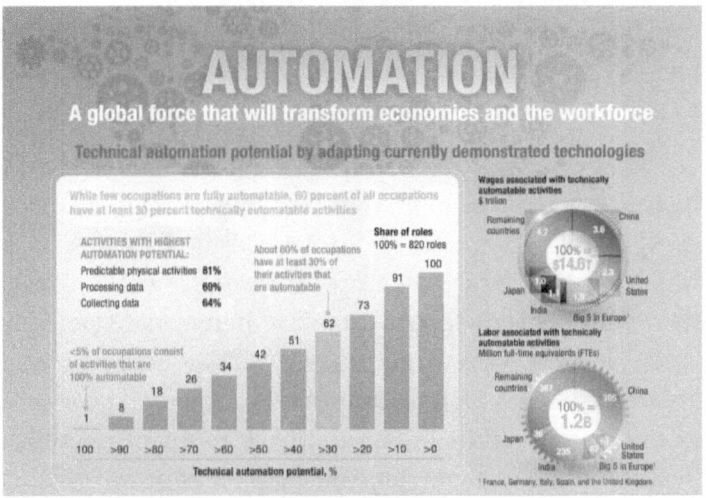

Also, according to McKinsey (Manyika, et al., 2017):

- 60 percent of all occupations have at least 30 percent technically automatable activities.

- Predictable physical activities have an 81 percent potential for automation.

- Data processing has a 69 percent potential for automation.

- Data collection has a 64 percent potential for automation.

Automation is not a thing of the future. For instance, the Tata Motors' plant in Pune, which manufactured its latest model, the Harrier, has moved to a module in which, over ninety percent of the manufacturing process is automated (Shah, 2018). There is certainly no exaggeration in the statement of Jim Yong Kim, President of the World Bank, when he said in 2016 that, *'Research based on World Bank data has predicted that the proportion of jobs threatened by automation in India is 69 percent, 77 percent in China and as high as 85 percent in Ethiopia'* (World Bank, 2016).

Analysing the data from the World Bank (World Bank, 2018), it is evident that every percentage increase in GDP in India creates about 7.5 lakh new jobs. So, for India to create between 1 crore–1.2 crore new jobs a year, the country needs to grow its GDP between 13 percent to 16 percent. Given the post-COVID-19 scenario, our growth is likely to fall to around two percent. So, we will need a massive shift in our approach to investment and business policies, to not only meet up the shortfall of jobs, but also create a robust economic model that can take us to 12–15% GDP growth in the next five years. Else, the jobs retention is going to be a perpetual problem.

I believe that there are economic opportunities for every service opportunity. Each sector will create at least a million new jobs. We need to quantify them, provide investment, and support them through an enabling ecosystem. I am not mentioning the entrepreneurial opportunities in this book as I have delved in detail about 58 entrepreneurial opportunities to create about 78 crore jobs in my other book titled, 'Your Vote is Not Enough' (Gupta R.P., Your Vote is Not Enough – Citizen's Charter to Making a Difference, 2019).

So, post the COVID shutdown, automation will inevitably get fast-tracked. Globally, the United Nations should revisit its Sustainable Development Goals (SDGs) and correct its mistake of ignoring 'automation' in sustainable development by adding another goal, SDG18 – 'Sustainable Automation.' Mad rush for automation will have a cascading effect, and this is not something the world is prepared for, given that we have 7.7 billion humans (United Nations, 2020) to cater to, and sustain. Sustainable Automation is where we need a better understanding of the business community and political leadership.

'Profits' with the 'proliferation of technology' should not be without 'people'! If we keep people out of the equation, the consequences would undermine all other SDGs and, maybe, render them irrelevant. It is time for the United Nations to have the most critical SDG, 'Sustainable Automation', as an 'intergenerational goal'.

'For India, the road ahead is much painful, unless we stall indiscriminate automation'.

For a country like India, we need to adopt 'Sustainable Automation' as an overarching goal and define its framework by forming an inter-ministerial group of: Ministry of HRD, Ministry of Science & Technology, Ministry of Labour & Employment, and Ministry of Electronics and Information Technology. This must be addressed as a focus area and as a high priority.

So, the **hard decision** is – not to adopt indiscriminate automation, but adopt a framework and implement 'Sustainable Automation.'

Urban Centric or Countryside

Our overly metro focused economic model has created a huge attraction and a big divide. The attraction is that, due to the focus on the metro's development, people migrate to metros in the hope of greener pastures. 43% of the population of Delhi and Mumbai are migrants (Ministry of Housing and Urban Poverty Alleviation, 2017). While here (in metros), their condition is not for the better always and there is a big divide created between the 'haves and have nots'. Now that we are building smart cities, it will further aggravate the divide amongst – smart cities, urban and rural. We have to take a step back and rethink what we are doing and whether this uneven growth of metro towns will do any good to these metro towns, or to the villages and towns from where the villagers will migrate? This model of development needs to change. We have to develop farmlands and create new economic hubs between farmlands and the districts in a planned manner, so that people start moving towards the countryside and we can decongest the towns. Also, with such a step, the property prices, which have shot up unrealistically, will come down to realistic levels. During COVID-19, one obvious point to note is that, the financial hubs were the worst hit – be it New York or Mumbai. Doesn't it appear strange to have separate Ministries of Urban Development and Rural Development?

So, it may be wiser to make a **hard decision** of de-risking our growth by not overly focusing on metro based financial hubs, and move to creating multiple financial hubs across zones in India and also focus more on movement towards the farmlands (countryside).

Wealth Distribution or Wealth Creation

'Wealth creation itself should be Wealth Distribution'

Every country's focus is on wealth creation, but the wealth creation, as I discuss in the section on the 'Distributed Growth Model', is happening only for a few, and then too, there are no long-term wealth creation strategies. In fact, those who have money are making more, and the divide between the rich and the poor is widening, with many economists claiming that if there is no wealth creation, there is no distribution! Well, they imply that if large corporates create wealth, they pay more taxes, and thus the government gets money to distribute. However, the facts are different. Bigger corporates know how to avoid paying taxes, and there are many ways in which they twist the 'system' and circumvent it. In fact, if we focused on the 'German Mittelstand' model mentioned earlier, *wealth creation itself should be wealth distribution*, because a large number of small enterprises would be creating wealth.

So, the **hard decision** is – to make a move to an economic model where wealth creation is wealth distribution, rather than relying on the trickle-down effect of distributing wealth from the taxes earned from large corporations.

Quantity or Quality & Innovation

While businesses ramp up production lines, they have an essential lesson to learn from China and Germany. Though China started as an imitator initially, but finally, China became the world's manufacturing hub, based on the quality and innovation of its products.

Similarly, Germany, where small and medium businesses drive the manufacturing, is all about quality, which makes it's produce the world's most-sought-after 'German Perfection'!

So, the **hard decision** here – is to focus on not just Quantity, but on Quality and Innovation. And, rather than being an imitator, be an innovator of products.

Following or Setting Standards

India has to learn quite a few things from the United States of America, the first thing is that, America sets the standards, and the world follows it, and that is why it is called a pioneer and a trend-setter. In every field, the USA has set standards, and its regulatory bodies are way ahead. Setting standards is a great business strategy – when you set standards, you create new businesses and since the standards are from the USA, the USA based companies take the lead, and bring out products, and thus rule the world markets. In my address to the regulators at the Indian Pharmacy Congress in December 2019, I suggested that, as regulators, they should not just look at the present issues and challenges, but imagine the future and prepare regulations for catalyzing business opportunities, keeping the user's interest as an overarching theme.

Let me give you an example of how, by setting our standards and that too, pioneering ones, we can build phenomenal business opportunities. Last year, at the Quality Council of India (an independent body under DIPP, Ministry of Commerce and Industry, Government of India), I suggested that we define the standards for 'Digital Health' and 'Care Homes and Hospices'. Since these standards don't exist, there is no accreditation of facilities. Imagine, once the NABH (National Accreditation Board for Hospitals & Healthcare) starts the accreditation based on the pre-defined standards. It is very likely that people will get into Digital Health and

Care Homes and Hospices. And I am quite optimistic these businesses will be set up in every town and will create at least a million jobs, if not more. Moreover, Digital Health Accreditation, being the first of its kind in the world, will set a new benchmark.

The way forward:

- Create a portal – www.standards.gov.in, and let every sector be listed. The standards in that sector are mentioned, and all organizations that are working on standards be mentioned. For example, on technology standards for health, the following ministries and departments have been working; 1) Telecom Engineering Centre under Ministry of Communications and Information Technology 2) National Health Systems Resource Centre under Ministry of Health and Family Welfare 3) NABH under DIPP, Ministry of Commerce and Industry and 4) Bureau of Indian Standards (BIS) under Ministry of Commerce and Industry. There could be more organizations as well, of which, I may not be aware. So, spending tax-payers money on doing overlapping and repetitive work in silos is uncalled for and not only wastes resources, but also creates confusion through multiple standards for similar services and products.

- Convert Bureau of Indian Standards into the Standards Development Institute with proper funding and infrastructure.

- India must not just be a follower of the International Harmonization task force on standards, but a pioneer in driving standards within India and sharing it with the world after a certain time lag, so that Indian companies have an edge for the use-case development and product development.

- Here, I would give an example of how the United States of America leads to defining the future, much ahead of time. In 1966, more than half a century ago, the USA commissioned a report titled, 'Technology and the American Economy' (Gupta R.P., Your Degree is Not Enough – Education for GenNext). So, the USA set a standard much before others, and then, their companies lapped on the opportunity to create business. The impact is visible in the Silicon Valley enterprises today, and how the USA has led the technology-driven enterprises. Today, if we see all the trillion-dollar enterprises from the USA; be it Alphabet (Google), Apple, Amazon, or Microsoft, the result of America's focus on 'Technology & the Economy' has given amazing result. Today, just these four trillion-dollar enterprises from the USA have a combined valuation of US$ 4 trillion, while the entire Indian Economy is about US$ 2.7 trillion. So, it does make sense for India to realise that, it cannot become a leader in technology without first leading the standards and regulation space.

In my earlier book, I made a point about India moving away from being a body shop of techies, to being an innovator, by creating an indigenous operating system, and other digital tools (Gupta R.P., Your Vote is Not Enough – Citizens Charter for Making a Difference, 2019, p. 49). During this time of COVID-19, imagine the security threat we have by using ZOOM and other video conferencing tools. Was a country of 1.35 billion not capable of creating such tools, or the policymakers failed to provide an ecosystem to achieve this easy goal?

So, clearly India has a **hard decision** to make – whether it wants to be a follower of world-class standards or set India class standards for the world. Time to change, and to get our priorities right, make hard decisions, and change our status as a follower of standards to setting new standards.

GDP or GDP per Capita

GDP of the oil-producing countries is high, but what about the GDP per capita? Because the oil wealth is limited to a few wealthy families, so, while GDP may be high, but it does not translate into a better quality of life or earnings for their residents. Also, similar is the case with export-oriented economies. India is looking at bringing manufacturers from China to India, and this is a good sign as it will bring in the FDI and also create a few thousand jobs, but not the millions of jobs that

India needs. Most of these companies are tech-driven, and they would use automation. The majority of the products will get exported – adding to the GDP and foreign reserves (which are essential), but the net impact on the population (GDP per capita) will not be higher. Consider this; if a company exports US$5 billion worth of products it makes through an automated plant like the 'Harrier' plant in Pune where 90% of the manufacturing is automated, what is the addition to the GDP per capita of the nation? Theoretically, yes, but practically – not really much. So, India has to focus on real GDP per capita income, and that will only happen through an inward-looking economy based on the 'Distributed Growth Model'.

Thus, the **hard decision** is in fact clear – our obsession with only GDP growth is wrong, and we need to look at creating more jobs and increasing GDP per capita.

Raising Taxes or Increasing Tax Payers

The biggest dilemma with the government is, how does it raise its financial resources – its tax collection immediately after the slowdown since 2019, and now given the lockdown due to COVID-19?

Recently, when some IRS (Indian Revenue Service) officers submitted a report about raising the taxes on the superrich – a pandemic cess, and higher levy on MNCs (PTI, Policy, 2020), the government expressed unhappiness about these unsolicited recommendations. This is not easy to implement, because if we raise more taxes, the companies will move to countries with lower tax regimes.

Historically, India is a 'Cash', 'Gold' and 'Property' investment economy, and it is going to be that way. The recent failure of multiple banks has created more doubt in the minds of people about keeping money in the bank. Demonetization didn't work, and any push to make India a digital or digital gold economy will not work in isolation. *Storing in gold and stocking cash is an old Indian psyche, and so, not that every cash stored in India is black money.* In fact, being a cash-driven economy was one of the key reasons why India was able to withstand the 2008–09 global economic crisis.

The way forward:

SAFER (Savings Assurance for Every Retiree)

Let us put a scheme that, anyone who is paying taxes, would be eligible for 6.0% of the total taxes paid as annual pension post the age of sixty, and farmers can be given a higher percentage, say 6.5 or 7%. Imagine if I paid Rs. 50 lakhs as taxes in my entire working life, and I get Rs. 3 lakh annual pension. Wouldn't I be happy to pay taxes? With incomes rising with India's growth story, both the amount paid as taxes, and income earned, could go up!

Post-COVID, this scheme could be launched. In effect, the tax payment would become like a deposit for 'post-retirement savings bank account', which pays after retirement at the rate of 6% per year for people other than farmers, who can get higher income. These deposits should be individual based and non-transferable. This scheme will let more and more people, including traders and self-employed, or even farmers, start paying taxes. India being predominantly a young country, will be able to take care of social security, and also secure the much-needed money to invest in India's growth. This scheme could be a real success story. Why would one not pay taxes honestly when s/he knows that s/he will get 6% of all the taxes paid as a recurrent pension every year? It would also show a caring face of the government and ROTP (Return On Taxes Paid). So, even a little higher tax rate would be good for citizens as they would be assured of some fixed financial security when they retire.

So, the **hard decision** is that, instead of increasing taxes, let us innovatively increase the tax-payers.

FPI, FII, FDI or DII

Foreign Portfolio Investors and Foreign Institutional Investors (FPI/FII) have invested massively in India, and the total investments are to the tune of US$178.28 Billion in India between FY02–20 (Till March 25, 2020)

In 2019, FPI investments in Indian equities touched a five-year high of Rs. 101,122 crore (IBEF, 2020)

If we look at the sector-wise FDI Equity inflows as per the Government of India data;

STATEMENT ON SECTOR-WISE FDI EQUITY INFLOWS FROM APRIL 2000 TO DECEMBER 2019

(PIB, 2020)

S.No	Sector	Amount of FDI Inflows		% age of Total Inflows
		(In Rs. crore)	(In US$ million)	
1	SERVICES SECTOR (Finance, Banking, Insurance, Non Finance/Business, Outsourcing, R&D, Courier, Tech. Testing and Analysis, Other)	462,114.07	80,670.79	17.66
2	COMPUTER SOFTWARE & HARDWARE	266,385.18	43,586.95	9.54
3	TELECOMMUNICATIONS	218,047.28	37,116.34	8.13
4	TRADING	168,426.20	26,541.60	5.81
5	CONSTRUCTION DEVELOPMENT: Townships, housing, built-up infrastructure and construction-development projects	121,888.63	25,371.47	5.55

S.No	Sector	Amount of FDI Inflows		% age of Total Inflows
		(In Rs. crore)	(In US$ million)	
6	AUTOMOBILE INDUSTRY	141,436.94	23,892.81	5.23
7	CHEMICALS (OTHER THAN FERTILIZERS)	97,134.96	17,441.95	3.82
8	DRUGS & PHARMACEUTICALS	87,066.62	16,396.56	3.59
9	CONSTRUCTION (INFRASTRUCTURE) ACTIVITIES	103,388.96	16,156.21	3.54
10	POWER	80,257.38	14,652.96	3.21
11	HOTEL & TOURISM	85,388.44	14,426.19	3.16
12	MISCELLANEOUS INDUSTRIES	60,260.44	11,618.93	2.54
13	METALLURGICAL INDUSTRIES	60,733.28	11,458.30	2.51
14	FOOD PROCESSING INDUSTRIES	60,349.12	9,781.00	2.14
15	NON-CONVENTIONAL ENERGY	56,235.56	9,100.76	1.99

S.No	Sector	Amount of FDI Inflows		% age of Total Inflows
		(In Rs. crore)	(In US$ million)	
16	INFORMATION & BROADCASTING (INCLUDING PRINT MEDIA)	51,829.62	8,713.38	1.91
17	ELECTRICAL EQUIPMENTS	50,018.69	8,506.97	1.86
18	PETROLEUM & NATURAL GAS	35,372.87	7,077.82	1.55
19	HOSPITAL & DIAGNOSTIC CENTRES	40,420.35	6,625.45	1.45
20	INDUSTRIAL MACHINERY	32,221.57	5,568.28	1.22
21	CONSULTANCY SERVICES	31,555.47	5,410.47	1.18
22	CEMENT AND GYPSUM PRODUCTS	29,322.06	5,280.70	1.16
23	SEA TRANSPORT	25,427.76	4,234.28	0.93
24	MISCELLANEOUS MECHANICAL & ENGINEERING INDUSTRIES	18,993.32	3,631.53	0.80
25	TEXTILES (INCLUDING DYED, PRINTED)	20,091.59	3,412.21	0.75

S.No	Sector	Amount of FDI Inflows		% age of Total Inflows
		(In Rs. crore)	(In US$ million)	
26	EDUCATION	19,016.02	3,005.06	0.66
27	RUBBER GOODS	17,901.21	3,002.74	0.66
28	FERMENTATION INDUSTRIES	15,759.08	2,794.97	0.61
29	MINING	15,076.29	2,655.48	0.58
30	ELECTRONICS	14,747.40	2,588.69	0.57
31	PRIME MOVER (OTHER THAN ELECTRICAL GENERATORS)	12,986.76	2,207.42	0.48
32	AGRICULTURE SERVICES	11,373.17	2,153.99	0.47
33	AIR TRANSPORT (INCLUDING AIR FREIGHT)	12,509.85	2,025.42	0.44
34	RETAIL TRADING	13,261.82	2,001.59	0.44
35	MEDICAL AND SURGICAL APPLIANCES	11,279.10	1,881.47	0.41

S.No	Sector	Amount of FDI Inflows		% age of Total Inflows
		(In Rs. crore)	(In US$ million)	
36	PORTS	6,730.91	1,637.30	0.36
37	SOAPS, COSMETICS & TOILET PREPARATIONS	9,363.65	1,589.52	0.35
38	PRINTING OF BOOKS (INCLUDING LITHO PRINTING INDUSTRY)	9,789.39	1,537.90	0.34
39	PAPER AND PULP (INCLUDING PAPER PRODUCTS)	7,889.62	1,449.63	0.32
40	DIAMOND, GOLD ORNAMENTS	6,817.75	1,172.94	0.26
41	RAILWAY RELATED COMPONENTS	6,353.58	1,070.93	0.23
42	MACHINE TOOLS	5,302.77	978.83	0.21
43	VEGETABLE OILS AND VANASPATI	5,805.00	977.98	0.21
44	CERAMICS	4,470.59	870.94	0.19
45	FERTILIZERS	3,908.51	687.87	0.15

S.No	Sector	Amount of FDI Inflows		% age of Total Inflows
		(In Rs. crore)	(In US$ million)	
46	GLASS	3,826.08	680.04	0.15
47	AGRICULTURAL MACHINERY	3,118.45	558.90	0.12
48	EARTH-MOVING MACHINERY	2,654.87	463.28	0.10
49	COMMERCIAL, OFFICE & HOUSEHOLD EQUIPMENTS	2,046.51	388.57	0.09
50	SCIENTIFIC INSTRUMENTS	1,690.61	280.14	0.06
51	BOILERS AND STEAM GENERATING PLANTS	1,624.24	263.37	0.06
52	SUGAR	1,279.47	213.83	0.05
53	LEATHER, LEATHER GOODS AND PICKERS	1,118.59	200.42	0.04
54	TIMBER PRODUCTS	1,074.35	182.39	0.04
55	TEA AND COFFEE (PROCESSING & WAREHOUSING COFFEE & RUBBER)	774.38	149.62	0.03

S.No	Sector	Amount of FDI Inflows		% age of Total Inflows
		(In Rs. crore)	(In US$ million)	
56	GLUE AND GELATIN	945.36	147.63	0.03
57	DYE-STUFFS	541.21	92.73	0.02
58	INDUSTRIAL INSTRUMENTS	452.29	88.23	0.02
59	PHOTOGRAPHIC RAW FILM AND PAPER	273.76	67.29	0.01
60	COAL PRODUCTION	119.19	27.73	0.01
61	DEFENCE INDUSTRIES	51.93	8.82	0.00
62	MATHEMATICAL, SURVEYING AND DRAWING INSTRUMENTS	39.80	7.98	0.00
63	COIR	22.05	4.07	0.00
	Grand Total	2,636,361.99	456,789.66	

In terms of sectoral investments, 35.33% of Foreign Direct Investment (FDI) was in soft infrastructure (technology-driven industries), which are not job intensive sectors. In fact, these sectors are probably having the highest valuation comparable to others sectors, so we know that the investors are in for valuations and quick ROI (Return On Investment), and such investors do not share India's vision for hard infrastructure and are guided by speculation-based valuation and invest and exit strategy. This trend is corroborated with the report from UNCTAD (United Nations Conference on Trade And Development), according to which, there is a substantially flat trend in terms of investments in the form of FDI and trade in goods, and much higher in services and international payment for intangibles (UNCTAD, 2019, p. 7).

While India may need foreign exchange reserves and much more in hard infrastructure where the investment is long-term, as also the vision, on the contrary, as is visible from the investments made by MNEs (Multi-National Enterprises), it is clear that they are investing in overseas markets with a lighter operation footprint, and that the asset-heavy MNEs in the top 100 are moving out in ranking or moving totally out of FDI (UNCTAD, 2019).

It is amply clear that FII/FDI don't align to our national priorities, and profits solely drive them. According to the World Investment Report 2019 from UNCTAD, Global Foreign Direct Investment flows have been sliding continuously due to the large scale repatriations of the accumulated foreign earnings by the United States MNEs in the first quarters of 2018, following the tax reforms introduced in the USA at the end of 2017 (UNCTAD, 2019, p. 7).

The repatriation of foreign earnings and investment in asset-light sectors shows both the strength and the weakness of the economic fundamentals. Also, with automation increasing over time, FDI investments will follow sectors that are not human resource-intensive and deliver high returns.

Hard infrastructure is human resource-intensive, and so, the government will have to take a call on whether we need the opportunistic investor – FII, FDI, or the government should make it a public good, or incentivize DII (Domestic Institutional Investors).

I wish to draw attention towards another trend that has picked up over a decade. Now, you can find bi-lateral or cross-sectoral program like INTEL-DST, Lockheed-Martin – DST etc. I simply don't understand why the government of India should join hands with such mega-corporations for consideration of a few million dollars! The government needs to understand the real agenda of these corporations. These large US-based corporations have hit a plateau on innovations, and they know that the next phase of innovations and path-breaking ideas would come from Universities and the developing world. So, they have created a small corpus, and tied up with various universities and governments, and invest or co-invest at an early-stage for innovative ideas. With this, they have access to the idea, and the Intellectual Property (IP), and at a later stage, if the idea takes off well, we all know who will be the real winner. India as a country, has to be really-really careful when it comes to ideating, nurturing, and scaling up innovations.

So, let us be clear about FIIs & FDI and not forget that, we are not like China, which holds about US\$3.06 trillion of foreign currency reserves (Xinhua, 2020). In comparison, the Indian economy is US\$2.74 trillion (UNCTAD, 2019). So, the only way we can break into the next league is based on innovative and self-funded research, and on our ability to commercialize the IP created. Else, we will keep getting ripped off of a few million dollars by following a partnership with big-brands, only to be swallowed later and losing our competitive advantage. We don't need such opportunistic external funding for such path-breaking ideas. It is a tough call but an important call. *'It is not just about the economy, it is about the internal stability and external influence'.*

So, the **hard decision** to make is – let's not totally depend on FII or FDI, but on DII.

Make in India or Customers for Make in India

Make in India is a great program, and with COVID-19, the world would have realised that India has been way ahead of the learning curve by launching this program.

For Make in India, corporates will invest in India, and for that to be sustainable, the government will have to ensure that there are enough customers with discretionary spending power to buy products made under the 'Make in India' program.

There is a **hard decision** to be made in this case, and it is that, without 'Customers' for 'Make in India', 'Make in India' will not reach its stated goals.

Investment Deficit or Fiscal Deficit

Currently, global rating agencies, bookish economists, and governments are concerned about a goal that goes against the interest of an LMIC—maintaining a fiscal deficit of not more than 3.3 percent. (Fiscal deficit is what occurs when the government's expenditure exceeds the revenue it generates. This revenue does not include the money which the government has borrowed).

Also, if we consider where the government gets its rupee and spends it (Ministry of Finance, Government of India, 2020), we will realise that it is a catch-22 situation for the government.

Where the Government gets its rupee

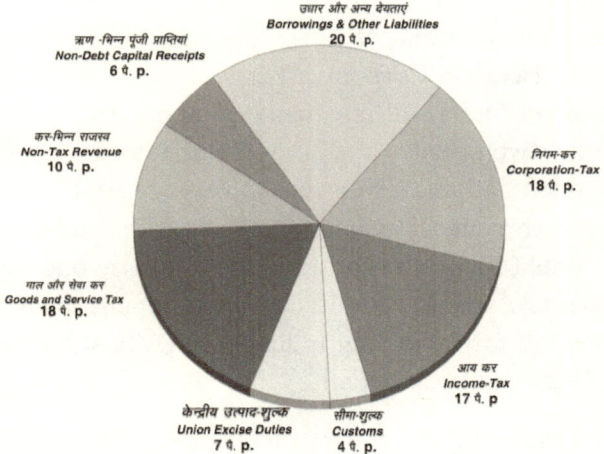

ऋण -भिन्न पूंजी प्राप्तियां
Non-Debt Capital Receipts
6 पै. p.

उधार और अन्य देयताएं
Borrowings & Other Liabilities
20 पै. p.

कर-भिन्न राजस्व
Non-Tax Revenue
10 पै. p.

निगम-कर
Corporation-Tax
18 पै. p.

माल और सेवा कर
Goods and Service Tax
18 पै. p.

आय कर
Income-Tax
17 पै. p

केन्द्रीय उत्पाद-शुल्क
Union Excise Duties
7 पै. p.

सीमा-शुल्क
Customs
4 पै. p.

Where the Government spends its rupee

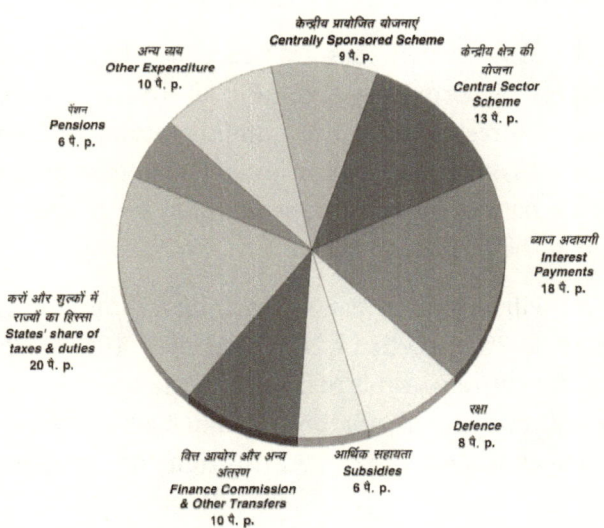

अन्य व्यय
Other Expenditure
10 पै. p.

केन्द्रीय प्रायोजित योजनाएं
Centrally Sponsored Scheme
9 पै. p.

केन्द्रीय क्षेत्र की
योजना
**Central Sector
Scheme**
13 पै. p.

पेंशन
Pensions
6 पै. p.

ब्याज अदायगी
**Interest
Payments**
18 पै. p.

करों और शुल्कों में
राज्यों का हिस्सा
**States' share of
taxes & duties**
20 पै. p.

वित्त आयोग और अन्य
अंतरण
**Finance Commission
& Other Transfers**
10 पै. p.

आर्थिक सहायता
Subsidies
6 पै. p.

रक्षा
Defence
8 पै. p.

It seems complicated for any government to garner funds needed to invest in massive CAPEX needed for infrastructure and job creation. Due to COVID-19, the income on account of GST, Customs, Union Excise, Income Tax, and Corporate Tax will go down by about 20 percent. India will remain a capital hungry nation for the next two decades if it has to break into the league of developed nations. Given that for every rupee spent by the government, 24 paise goes to subsidies and interest payments (6 paise on subsidies and 18 paise on interest payments), would the Indian government have any money left for rebuilding India post COVID-19, without breaching our fiscal deficit?

Considering that the businesses were already reeling under a severe slowdown since 2019, and now, with COVID-19 driven lockdown for about two months, it will have a debilitating effect on businesses of all sizes – smaller the business, larger the impact.

The Government has to figure out how to invest massively in providing capital and finance, building infrastructure, running the administration, and social security, to create and sustain enough jobs, even factoring the international workforce which may be headed back home in the next two years.

We will have to invest, so the Indian economy jumps back to 6–7% growth in 2021 and over 10% by 2022. Since the entire world is reeling with the same economic crises, India should not bother much about what the rating agencies have to say. At this time, it is prudent for the government to breach its fiscal deficit numbers and invest massively in infrastructure.

As long as money is a capital investment towards creating infrastructure, both hard and soft, why should we be worried about a goal like maintaining a 3.3 percent fiscal deficit? The deficit can be 5 percent or even 7 percent, but what India needs at present is massive investments in the farmland, MSMEs, SHGs, migrant labourers, education, skills development, and healthcare.

So far, in all our economic policies, the long term wealth creation has been missing. We need to invest massively in sectors with multiplier effects like; agriculture, tourism, restaurants, education, health, construction, MSME, and entertainment.

We need to identify the demand and supply perspectives from primary (agriculture, fishing, mining), secondary (finished goods-manufacturing) and tertiary sectors (services which help secondary sectors like; logistics, insurance, warehousing, tourism, entertainment, financial services, teaching, and healthcare, etc.), and simultaneously concentrate on building the circular economy to keep the carbon footprint in check, and also leverage the massive economic opportunity of the green economy, as we embark on double-digit growth, which should be responsible and sustainable from an inter-generational perspective.

All the above mentioned may not require massive investments. Still, some of them will need funds for up-gradation, which will immediately create jobs, boost economic activity, increase tax collection, and massively uplift growth to the extent of doubling it from where it was in FY'19. Why do we suffocate growth by creating an 'investment deficit' and keep concentrating on maintaining the fiscal deficit? In my view, prudence lies in tilting the balance and avoiding an investment deficit today to ensure that we have a budgetary surplus tomorrow. The need of the hour is a massive upliftment of basic amenities, and it is time that we avoid the prescriptions given to us by both – the International Monetary Fund and the World Bank. We have already paid a heavy price by borrowing economists from the World Bank, the IMF, and other leading global forums and universities to guide us. It is now time to look inwards and develop an indigenous growth model. We must not ever lose sight of the fact that powerful countries have many tools—which they conveniently call independent, or have multi-lateral agencies—through which they directly or indirectly pressurize developing economies to stifle their plans and growth. We must note that rating agencies such as Moody's or Standard and Poor's cannot drive the collective future of such a massive population. It is essential that the 'Developing World' lives by its definitions and criteria and not those defined by the developed world's rating agencies. The time is upon us to work towards proposing a currency for the developing world, which should be added to foreign currency reserves and for international trading. Dollar-denominated trading does not work for the developing world. It is time also that India takes the lead in creating an organization that works for the developing world, unlike the WTO, which majorly caters to the developed world. According to the World Bank (World Bank, 2020), based on the Gross National Income (GNI) per capita, there are 31 Low-Income Economies and 47 Lower – Middle Income Economies. India should play a stewardship role in galvanizing all these 78 countries to propose a new group *'D-78'* (developing economies) and collaborate for mutually beneficial opportunities to uplift their populations.

So, the **hard decision** is, it's better not to have 'Investment Deficit' and live with 'Fiscal Deficit' for the next few years, and not suffocate investments, growth and development.

Economic Growth or Economic Development

One fact is crystal clear—the value of the nation's currency not only mirrors the strength of its economy, it is directly proportional to it. In my opinion, there is a big difference between economic growth and economic development.

Economic development is a broader concept, which includes, GDP per capita, and other indicators like; poverty alleviation, social justice, income distribution, health, education, pollution, and equality of income. It also reflects how income is spent.

Economic growth only indicates a narrow concept of national income. The actions of successive governments are overly focused on economic growth, represented by the GDP, and if we are to adopt economic development in its broadest sense, I think it will be appropriate to rename the Ministry of Finance as the Ministry of Economic Development.

So, the **hard decision** is, to focus on economic development and not get obsessed with economic growth.

Incremental or Exponential Growth

India as a country, is at an inflection point due to the following considerations;

- 65 percent of the country's population is below 35 years in age and the average age of the population is 29 years.

- The demographic dividend will only last for the next 25 years, so whatever growth or productivity we need to achieve, we have to do it in the next twenty-five years.

- We need to keep the growth in high double digits to keep India as an attractive investment destination.

- Considering the fact that, every percent growth in GDP creates 7.5 lakh jobs in India, we will need to grow at 16% per year to create 1.2 crore jobs needed every year to absorb the new entrants into the job market.

- Also, if we consider the GDP growth per capita required for India to become a developed country in the next twenty-five years, we need an annual GDP per capita growth of 15.81%.

Given the current situation of our growth and our need to meet the aspirations of youth and keep them gainfully employed, 7–8 percent growth will be considered incremental and will not suffice. We need to grow exponentially, around 16% per year.

So, the **tough decision** is a Hobson's choice, we need to grow around 16% per year. Now, it is not about incremental growth, but about exponential growth.

Globalization or Glocalization

We all know for a fact, that the world will not be the same again post COVID-19. Champions and supporters of Globalization will take a step back. People who saw China rising as a polarizing super-power will rethink. America can never be great again! America was great – not because it was big, but it was big because it was great, and it led the world and championed the cause of security, growth, and equality, based on certain beliefs. One may have questioned the beliefs, but yes, it had some principles for its conduct.

America, where it stands today, has created a vacuum, which is hard to fill in, as America has prevailed upon the world due to its consumer's buying power, US dollar as the global currency, and its military prowess. It is a new world, and every country around the globe will have to recalibrate its position and foreign relations. COVID-19 also has reset the global supply chains, which means that countries like China, the United States of America, and India stand to feel the most impact. Whether the impact will be positive or negative depends on the speed and scope, sector-wise recalibration, policy directions, investments, and speed of execution. It would need bold thinking and fearless execution on foreign and commercial policies, including taxation.

China could have been a net gainer post-COVID-19, but for that to happen, it needs a different game-plan, and that I don't see in the making as of now and moreover, with global powers ganging up against China, it is on a slippery slope. So, countries like the United States of America and India, can quickly move up the ante and fill in the 'trust vacuum'. It depends on how well we manage the COVID-19. Also, for the United States of America, it's the election year, and Trump will do all within his ambit to win, and the only way to do this is, to bring back the manufacturing to the United States and create jobs. No other thing guarantees him a victory. So, post the COVID-19 era, it means action from the two – the oldest, and the largest democracy, to pull the business by all means. The USA is a business-friendly country, where the top bureaucracy comes and goes with the President, meaning that, the administration is aligned to the leader at the helm. In India, bureaucracy acts as a bottleneck and will remain a stumbling block for India to become proactive and agile in such an environment. So, four possible scenarios may emerge in terms of global manufacturing repositioning;

- *China plus strategy*. This implies having another country besides China as a manufacturing base. Major global giants will likely adopt this strategy. India and other countries in Asia will gain, in the process to wean away a few large companies to shift their manufacturing base from China. India may benefit due to a stable government at the centre.

- *China minus strategy*. This means not having China as a manufacturing base. Still, it is unlikely for some companies with major consumption in China considering the business-friendly environment and availability of human resources, besides the convenience to export to countries in South East Asia and the Pacific region.

- *Back to the USA*. USA will put all within its might to force USA head-quartered giants to shift the manufacturing to the USA.

- *Broaden the base in the ASEAN region*. It is a fact that the countries which are relatively small in size have snapped manufacturing from China and gained in the past, and they may gain more post-COVID-19. The countries which stand to gain are Vietnam, Thailand, Malaysia, Indonesia, Philippines, and Singapore.

Given the scenarios mentioned above, India has to do a lot more to make the best of the opportunity. A critical human resource parameter to focus is that, when it comes to the highest worker productivity, Malaysia beats all ASEAN countries with a GDP per worker at US$49,000 which is more than double that of China at US$21,000 per worker (Upton, 2019).

So, unless we develop the worker's productivity and a business-friendly administration, it is likely that in the fight between China and the World, India does not benefit the most, and it could be the rest of the ASEAN nations. This is a once in a lifetime opportunity for India. We have to move swiftly. Though, I am not sure if, with the current bureaucratic setup, we will be able to leverage the opportunity to the fullest. PMO may handle this opportunity efficiently, but when it comes to the local experience dealing with various offices, nothing much changes, and it puts off many investors. It is essential to address the issue if we want the system to handle the workload and deliver it. It cannot be a person-centric system that can be depended on for such an opportunity.

Let us keep this in mind that the first two world wars were a great leveller for the business world and also set the new world order. COVID-19 is the third world war in a real sense. In this, the weapon fired is invisible and the definition of world war has changed from a military to a trade war.

It is time for India to create an inward-looking model that is based on MSMEs, agriculture, SHGs, and traders. We would certainly need to focus on manufacturing and exports. Ideally, exports should be around 20 percent but never cross more than 25% of the GDP.

So, the **hard decision** for India is, to move towards glocalization, keeping a focus on our core economic strengths – Agriculture and MSMEs, and exports based on the them i.e – 'Glocalization model'.

Giant Leap Forward

The 'Giant Leap Forward' in India's march towards development will be the shift from the old paradigm to the new paradigm, as a sum up of the tough choices involved and the hard decision to be made.

No.	Old Paradigm	New Paradigm
1	Lobbying for Policy Making	Crowd Sourcing Policy Inputs
2	Small Number of Large Companies	Large Number of Small Companies
3	Making Agriculture Profitable	Making Agriculture an Attractive Business
4	Genetically Modified and Chemical Farming	Organic Farming
5	Loan Waiver	Loan Deferment
6	Energy Generation	Renewable Energy & Conservation
7	Divesting PSUs	Building SPSUs
8	Automation	Sustainable Automation
9	Urban Centric	Countryside model
10	Wealth Distribution	Wealth Creation
11	Quantity	Quality & Innovation
12	Following Standards	Setting Standards
13	GDP	GDP per capita

No.	Old Paradigm	New Paradigm
14	Raising Taxes	Increasing Tax Payers
15	FPI, FII & FDI	DII
16	Make in India	Customers for Make in India
17	Investment Deficit	Fiscal Deficit
18	Economic Growth	Economic Development
19	Incremental Growth	Exponential Growth
20	Globalization	Glocalization

India's Biggest Challenge is the Greatest Opportunity

The Missing Middle-Class

While successive governments have sold the 'India Story' based on the buying power of the 1.3+ billion Indians, it was more about the Middle-class Indian story. But what defines the middle-class, and how many middle-class people are there in India? Have we looked deeper into the middle-class and identified them, and their buying power? The direction which the Indian Economy will take will depend on the buying power of the middle class, but there are many gaps in this story. Also, once we have identified it, we need to convert this into one of the strong fundamentals of our economy.

First, middle-class or middle-income, are used synonymously, and there are various versions of what constitutes the middle-class. According to The National Council of Applied Economic Research (NCAER), the middle class comprises of two sub-groups: 'Seekers' with an annual household income between Rs. 200,000 and Rs. 500,000, and 'Strivers' with an annual household income between Rs. 500,000 to Rs. 10,00000 at 2001/2002 prices.

Banerjee and Duflo (2008) have defined the new middle class as those who spend between $2 and $10 per capita per day (1993 PPP). Within the new middle class, they further classify two categories of households: the lower middle class, whose daily per capita expenditures are between $2 and $4, and the upper-middle class. The expenditures of the latter lie between $6 and $10. (Krishnan & Hatekar, Rise of the New Middle Class in India and Its Changing Structure, 2017, p. 41).

One analysis pegs the middle-class at 60.4 crores in 2011–12 (Krishnan & Hatekar, Rise of the New Middle Class in India and Its Changing Structure, 2017, p. 42).

According to the Mastercard Center for Inclusive Growth (Wong), the middle-class annual household income is INR 151,651, and there are 1.64 crore middle-class households. Taking an average family size of 5.1, this will make the middle-class population to 8.3 crores.

A technical paper from the Center for Global Development (Meyer & Birdsall, 2012), estimates India's middle class at about ten crores.

So, there is no clear definition of middle-income or middle-class, and neither a definite number about the middle-class population. The variation in the available estimates is too high. It is high time the Indian government agrees to an acceptable definition of the middle-class. Also, the government should discontinue the decennial census (occurring every ten years) and start a triennial census (occurring every three years) for the economic and demographic profile, given the availability of digital tools in the fast-moving world. Also, going forward, we should consider doing away with the physical visits for census.

Validating the actual number of Middle-Class

I looked at multiple data sets to arrive at the approximate number of middle-class populations. I am of the view, and it will not be easy to digest, that we probably 'oversold' the India story by a relatively high margin. Now, we have to find the ways and means to address this challenge and convert it into our biggest opportunity.

So, let us look at the following numbers;

Credit Cards & Middle Class

As of January 2020, according to the Reserve Bank of India, the total number of credit cards issued (outstanding after adjusting the number of cards withdrawn/cancelled) is 56120245 (Reserve Bank of India, 2020). So, we have a total of 5.61 crore credit cards in India. Taking into account that people hold multiple credit cards, and also some people don't keep credit cards and also that people besides the middle class (affluent or HNIs) are included in this figure, if we go by the assumption that middle-class people are those who hold credit cards and take the entire number of credit cardholders as a middle-class, then, the middle class population is about 5.6 crore. If we factor the average family size assuming that the primary earner has the credit card and beneficiary family can be counted as middle class, then the total number is 5.6 × 5.1 (average family size), adding to 28.56 crores.

Two and Four wheelers & Middle-Class

The data of vehicle registrations since 1951 is another eye-opener. If we consider that people who have two-wheelers are in the middle-class, then the total registered vehicles in India since 1951 are 16.89 crores. If we factor the vehicle's average lifespan of 15 years and take two-wheelers from 2001 till 2016 (date till which the latest official data is available), then the number of two-wheelers would be about 13.04 crore. The number of 13.04 crore also includes people having more than one two-wheeler. But, even if we take this number without factoring families having more than one two-wheelers, the number of the middle-class does not go beyond 13.04 crores, and if we add the factor of the family size of 5.1, then the total comes to 66.50 crores.

If we take four-wheelers as criteria for the middle-class and consider the vehicle's average lifespan of 15 years, then the total number of four-wheelers from 2001–2016 are 2.31 crore. The number of 2.31 crore also includes families having more than one four-wheeler and also includes jeeps and taxis. Still, if we take this figure without discounting taxis and multiple family holding, and factor it with an average family size of 5.1, the number of middle-class populations by definition of those having a four-wheeler does not cross 11.78 crores.

India: Composition of Vehicle Population (1951–2016)

As on 31st March	All vehicles	Two – wheelers *	Cars, Jeeps, and Taxis	Buses @	Goods Vehicles	Others**
2001	54,991,000	38,556,000	7,058,000	634,000	2948,000	5,795,000
2016	2,30,031,000	1,68,975,000	30,242,000	1,757,000	10,516,000	18,541, 000

*Two-wheelers include auto-rickshaws for the years ending 31st March 1959, 1960, 1962, 1964, 1965, 1967, 1968 and 1969. For the other years, auto-rickshaws are included in 'others.'

**Others include tractors, trailers, three-wheelers (passenger vehicles)/LMV, and other miscellaneous vehicles for which category wise break up is not reported by States/UT.

@Includes omni buses since 2001

The total may not tally due to rounding off data

Source: Offices of State Transport Commissioners/UT Administrators

Please note: All the figures above include historical data of registered vehicles since 1951–2016

(Government of India, Ministry of Road Transport & Highways, 2016, p. 33)

Let us now move to a few international comparisons.

Vehicles per capita in Developing nations

A very interesting data points towards our spending capacity vis a vis other developing nations of much smaller size and Australia:

Vehicular Penetration during 2014 of Selected Countries				
Country	Population in 2014 #	Per 1000 persons		
		Passenger cars	Total Motor Vehicles	Motor cycles and Mopeds
Developing Countries				
China	136.43 crore	76*	93*	70*
India	129.56 crore	19*	28*	102*
Brazil	20.28 crore	233	299	112
Mexico	12.04 crore	209	285	18
South Africa	5.45 crore	122	178	7
Malaysia	2.99 crore	382	421	389
Developed Country				
Australia	2.35 crore	567	718	33

*Pertains to data for 2013

data from other sources and this population chart has been inserted instead of GDP per capita for comparing populations and vehicle ownership.

Note: Passenger cards – motor vehicle, other than motor cycle, intended for the carriage of passengers and designed to seat no more *than nine persons (including the driver); Total motor vehicles – include passenger cars, buses, motor coaches, vans and lorries, but exclude motor cycles and mopeds; Motor cycles and moped – two or three-wheeled road motor vehicle not exceeding 400 kg of unladen weight.*

Sources: Data including that of India are from World Road Statistics, 2016, International Road Federation, Geneva (Government of India, Ministry of Road Transport & Highways, 2016, p. 17).

So, from a credit card data of 5.6 crores to four-wheelers ownership of 2.31 crores and two-wheeler data of 13.04 crores, the variations are mind-boggling. When we compare this data with the vehicle ownership of a country like Australia with a population of just 2.35 crore, having 718 vehicles per 1000 people, India has only 28 vehicles per 1000 people. So, our effective population of middle-class or those having the spending capacity to own two or four wheelers falls way short to justify that we have middle-class between 15–20 crores on the higher side – though it is hard to pinpoint the actual number of middle-class, considering the variations between various data.

Now, let us look at the next data sets of FDI investment in India and other countries to gauge the effective population size through their buying power.

Foreign Direct Investment (FDI)

India is a country with 1.35 billion population and let us now compare the FDI in India versus countries with much smaller population but with equal or comparative FDI investment based on the data from the United Nations Conference on Trade And Development (UNCTAD):

FDI & Population (2018)		
Country	FDI inflows (In US$ millions)	Population (In millions)
China	139043	1427
India	42285*	1352
Brazil	61223	209
Mexico	31604	126
South Africa	5334*	57
Spain	43590	46
Malaysia	8090	31
Australia	60438	24
Source: (UNCTAD, 2019) *Asset/liability basis		

FDI in a country is based on the earning potential of its population. India's largest state in terms of population is Uttar Pradesh, with a projected population of approximately 23 crores in 2020. Now, if we consider the size of Brazil (population of 20.90 crores), Mexico (population of 12.6 crores), Spain (population of 4.6 crores), and Australia (population of 2.4 crores) in the table above on the FDI, we will have some revealing insights mapping the FDI received ;

- India received US$42 Bn in 2018 and Brazil received US$61 Bn and Brazil is roughly the size of Uttar Pradesh.

- Mexico received FDI to the tune of US$ 32 Bn and is about half the size of Uttar Pradesh.

- Spain received an FDI of US$ 44 Bn with a population of about 4.6 crore, which is like 1/4th the size of Uttar Pradesh, and

- Australia received FDI of US$60 Bn, and its size is about 1/10th of Uttar Pradesh.

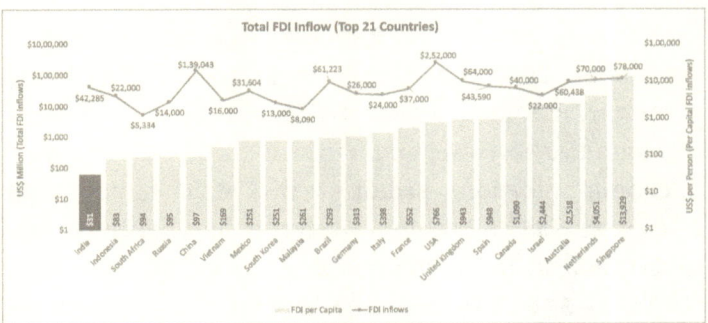

If we look at the global FDI inflows in the top 21 economies for the years 2017 and 2018 (UNCTAD, 2019), India received the lowest FDI per capita, as is evident from the chart above. We know that FDI comes primarily because of the buying power of the country's population. So, effectively, if we draw a comparison of India's real or effective population with buying power, and compare it to various countries that received FDI, and analyse this data along with the data on other domestic and international indicators, we can assume that we have an effective population (with buying capacity or spending power) roughly on a lower side of 3 crores and a maximum of 16 crores.

The sectors in India which get the maximum FDI

The technology sector got maximum FDI (Suneja, 2019), and then too, the FDI in India has happened not due to the Indian population's buying power, but because of investors taking advantage of special investment privileges due to lower wages and tax exemptions (IBEF, 2020). Also, during January – December 2019, the services sector attracted the highest FDI equity inflow of US$6.52 billion, followed by computer software and hardware – US$ 6.34 billion, telecommunications sector – US$ 4.29 billion, and trading at US$3.52 billion. Even the most recent mega-investment in India, the investment of US$ 5.7 billion or Rs. 43,574 crore for a 9.99% stake in Reliance Jio by Facebook (Fisher & Mohan, 2020), is in the tech sector. A minute analysis of FDI also indicates what our strengths and weaknesses are. Prima Facie, we need to build strong fundamentals of the economy which are missing. One key strong fundamental of the Indian economy should be the domestic consumption story based on the middle-class, the others being infrastructure, skilled human resources, availability of capital and law enforcement, broad spread of wealth generators like farmers and MSME etc.,.

Reality check: India falls in the middle rung of Lower Middle-Income Country!

India aspires to be a Middle-Income Country, but in reality, as of now, we are way below, and stand in the middle rung of the Lower-Middle Income class countries (LMIC), according to the latest World Bank's income group classification by income level (Gross National Income per Capita at current US$ – July 2019) for the fiscal year 2020 (World Bank, 2019) as ;

1. High income (Above US$12,375).

2. Upper-Middle Income (US$ 3996–12375).

3. Lower-Middle Income (US$1026–3995).

4. Low income (Under US$1026).

According to the IMF, India's GDP per capita was US$ 2198 at current prices in April 2019, and is projected to be US$2378 in 2020 (International Monetary Fund (IMF), 2019). But due to COVID-19, it might actually go lower. The chart below illustrates India's position with regards to GDP per capita when compared with some select economies (2018).

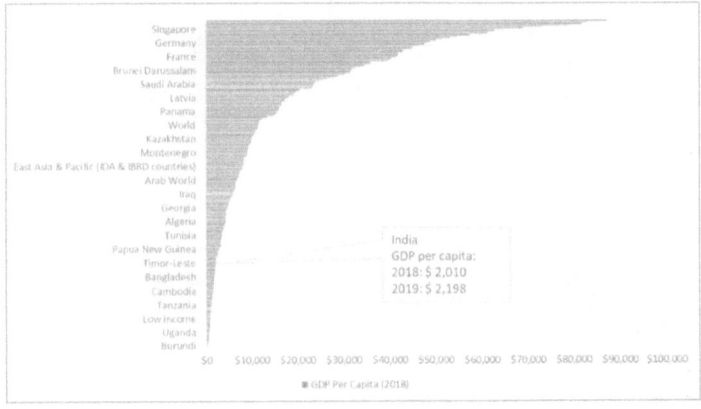

If we map India's GDP per capita as per the Lower-Middle Income Country classification defined as countries with GDP per capita between US$1026–3995, we are in the middle and not even in the top three of Lower-Middle Income Countries. Compare this to China; its GDP per capita is USD10,870 and the USA's GDP per capita is US$ 67430, according to IMF (2020) (Gupta R.P., Your Degree is Not Enough: Education for GenNext, 2020, p. 192). If we consider FDI and other indicators mentioned above, one thing is clear – we are way off the mark as a robust economy, and lacking the fundamentals needed to strengthen the Indian economy.

Action Plan to Move Forward

The chart below gives an indicative representation of the desired per capita GDP growth rate India needs to grow at for the next 25 years to move outside the LMIC category, to achieve the Upper-Middle Income category, high-income category and for achieving the OECD average, the world average, and the growth rate of the European Union.

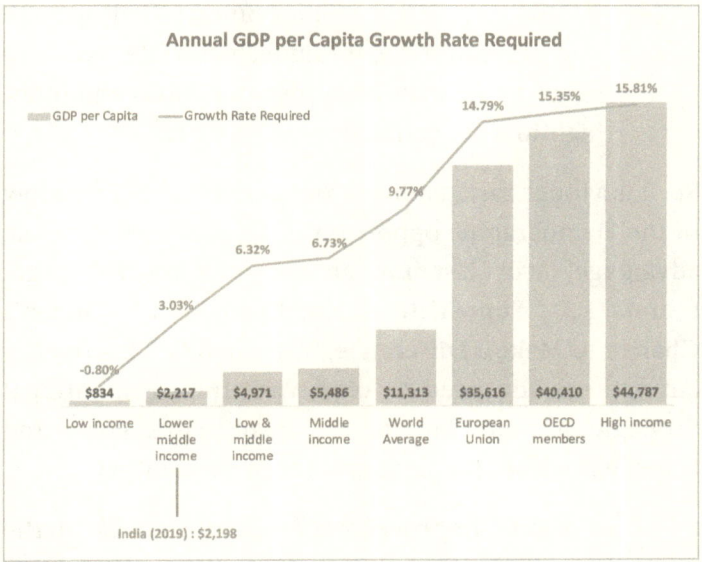

- The world's per capita GDP is growing at 3% average. In this analysis, it is assumed that the per capita GDP brackets would move up by 3% annually over the next 25 years.

- If India's GDP were not to grow at all, India would become a low-income group country.

- To remain in the current band of Lower-Middle-Income group, India must grow at 3% annually.

- At the current GDP per capita growth rate of 5%–7%, the best India can become is a middle-income group country.

- To reach the global GDP per capita average, India must grow at 9.77% for 25 years continuously.

- A 15% annual per capita annual GDP growth rate is required continuously for 25 years to climb to the likes of European nations and other high-income countries.

So, it is a tough task, taking into account that our window of the 'demographic opportunity,' i.e., our demographic advantage, will last for another twenty-five years (Gupta R.P., Your Vote is Not Enough – A Citizen's Charter to Make a Difference, 2019, p. 87). This further strengthens the need to create an 'Inter-generational Strategic Action Plan' to set quantifiable goals and achieve it within the next quarter of the century.

If we didn't improve our economic status in the next quarter of the century, we will be left with a skewed 'dependency ratio' (this ratio is a measure which shows the number of dependents, aged between zero and fourteen and those above the age of 65 years – to the total population segment aged between fifteen and sixty-four). We will not have enough income to support the aging population and feed our population, which will be about 1.69 billion in 2045 (Population, 2020), with an average life expectancy of 74.2 years (PTI, Poltics and Nation, 2017).

Most importantly, the senior citizens would be approximately 20% of our population numbering 338 million (PTI, Politics and Nation, 2019), and given that senior citizens earn less and have to spend more because of the state of their health and other needs, so clearly, it would put our nation in a state of demographic disadvantage if we didn't grow fast enough.

So, India has to set economic goals for the next twenty-five years and break it down into yearly goals and monitor them every six months, if not three months, to avoid a catastrophe in the next decade. We have no time to lose.

When we march on our inter-generational plan, we will also need to bring a drastic change in our outlook and how we handle issues, our work culture, and how we respond to success and failures. While systems are easy to change, but mindsets are difficult to change, and we need to change both simultaneously. If we don't change our approach, nothing much is expected to change.

Cultural Change and a Mindset Change

Change of Culture – Our Approach

COVID-19 brought the entire nation together, and proved to the world again that, whenever a national crisis descends, India will forget all the differences and come together as one nation and stand with the leader. But when the crisis is gone, we are back to the same – again, wanting for camaraderie till the next crisis hits us. Be it independence movement or Kargil or COVID-19, time and again, we have proven that only a crisis can unite us. The same has been our attitude and habit – we never worry till we are nearing a deadline – be it a task in office, or at home, or an examination, or an election. The action starts when we are near to the deadline. We must change this. We need to be professional and need to plan and do work diligently.

Meritocracy instead of sycophancy or favouritism: Another significant change we need in our culture is that, we need to pick people based on what they know and not whom they know. In practice, the criteria based on which the people are chosen for a job is based on sycophancy and favours they do; mostly, it is based on 'give and take culture.' If this continues, we will increasingly become a mediocrity based nation full of incompetent people. Currently, we are shocked to see a competent and honest person in the job as it is an exception to have an honest person in an entirely 'fixed system'. If someone makes in by chance, one is either cornered or adapts to the prevailing practices.

So, starting at the highest level, the most competent people need to be selected, so that this percolates down as a trickle-down effect. We must not forget that the culture is about the 'top man' in the system. If the top man is punctual, the entire team is punctual. If the top man is lazy or 'easy go types', the whole team behaves so. So, we need to emphasize on picking the right person leading every organization!

> *'Appreciating systemic problems, and making jokes on it, not only leads to accepting the practice as a part of our culture, but also promotes it'.*

If you see what goes on in our routine discussions, what should have been a serious topic of concern (corruption, lethargy, and non-performance), we have started appreciating these problems and also making jokes about them, and so, we have inadvertently made them socially acceptable behaviours, which should actually have been a taboo. We have reached a point where people have even become cynical about a positive change in their lifetime! We need to change this culture of accepting failures, lethargy, corruption and non – performance. If we don't do and only keep appreciating problems, we will keep getting them more, and personally, each one will suffer and also will keep paying a heavy price for appreciating such practices. So, it is time to give up this culture of appreciation and acceptance and change it to admonishment and rejection for things like corruption, lethargy, and non-performance.

We need to change our culture and become more objective and professional and not mix work and performance with any other consideration. We should deliver what is expected of us. This will help us in achieving our national goal of making India a developed country.

Mindset Change

Problem is not just about money; it is more about our mindset

Money or capital is not as much of a problem as making the best use of what is available, and trust me, India as a country is blessed with enough resources. Like for example, a Union Ministry had about rupees thirty thousand crores collected as cess, which was lying with it and it did not know what to do with it? It had to call a national level meeting to find a solution. Suggestions which were appreciated and welcomed have not been implemented despite more than two years having passed. So, here money was not a problem; it was a mindset of not doing anything till the Supreme court issued a notice!

Deaths of hundreds of children in Uttar Pradesh and Rajasthan in the past years due to the shortage of ventilators have not shaken our system, and no one even at the centre bothered to check with other states if they were prepared in case of such an eventuality? Had this been attended to, today, due to COVID-19, we would not be scrambling for want for ventilators. According to a recently held review meeting at the highest level in the government, and data being as recent as 23rd April 2020;

- 183 districts have less than 100 isolation beds, and of these districts, 67 have had COVID-19 cases.

- 123 districts have zero ventilator beds, and of these districts, 39 have COVID-19 cases.

- 143 districts have zero ICU beds, and of these districts, 47 have COVID-19 cases.

- In Uttar Pradesh, 53 out of 75 districts have fewer than 100 isolation beds, and of these, 31 have COVID-19 cases (Ghose, 2020).

Despite having enough warnings, and COVID-19 being declared 'High Risk' by WHO at the end of January, what were we waiting for? We have to be realistic in assessing the performance of the people at the helm of departments and organizations and we have to be ruthless to manipulators or non-performers. After deaths of infants in Gorakhpur in 2017 (PTI, LiveMint, 2017) and hundred plus children dying at a government hospital in Kota, Rajasthan in December 2019 and January 2020 (Reuters, 2020), we waited for COVID19 to strike the world with thousands of deaths to wake this nation about the need of ventilators! WHO Situations Reports (WHO, 2020) on a daily basis were conveying the ground reality in no uncertain terms, and very clearly since January 2020. Let us have a glance at the data in the table below;

Timeline	Spread (Countries)	Cases	Deaths
20th January	4	282	NA
20th February	27	7548	2129
20th March	About 150	234073	9840

(WHO, 2020)

Those who looked at the daily statistics could have easily figured out the speed of spread, as is evident from the table above. On 30th January, WHO declared COVID-19, 'A Public Health Emergency of International Concern' (Gupta R.P., Note from a Policy Maker, 2020). The moment COVID-19 spread from 4 to 27 countries in a month, India should have decided to stop all international flights. But the question is, will we take action and hold the officials responsible for such a major lapse? The nation has paid a heavy price for the failure of the officials responsible to evaluate, comprehend, and make appropriate recommendations timely. Since such officials are not held accountable for their omissions, the mindset and culture both have accepted that, nothing will happen and – 'sab chalta hai'. Officials who messed up and stalled all the projects of digital health, which could have come in handy at this hour of need, should be held accountable and stripped of their roles and let go. But since accountability is missing in the administration, the nation keeps paying a heavy price and also lags in development.

As Indians, we have to stop giving in to our emotions and start focusing on delivery, outcomes and success, and not on processes, activity, and emotions. For long, we have considered our affiliations to the birthplace, caste, religion, and friendship of all hues, to cloud our thinking and response, and this has resulted in mediocrity being a norm, instead of meritocracy. Further, this has been complicated by the social media. We are too lazy to verify the facts and we get carried away by reading the headlines and keep hoping that someone will take action, so why worry! It is time that every Indian starts to get directly involved in the governance of India. Voting is a starting point, but just voting is not enough. Our work starts much before voting and continues thereafter.

Look at things objectively – Whether a particular program will benefit the nation and most importantly, 'How' and 'By When' and 'What is the amount of

Tax Payer's money it involves? Unless we value our money and its deployment, we cannot take this nation forward. Every minute you spend to read this book or any newspaper or watch news, you are investing your most valuable resource – 'Time' and also, your 'Money' (Taxes you pay directly or indirectly). Remember, what Government spends is not its own money. It is the money it collects from people like you and me. We have to fix accountability for failures, and question if wrong decisions are taken, or officials and ministers who are working on our money (taxes) behave arrogantly or don't deliver on the roles they are appointed for.

Observe – Read – Think – Analyse – Take Action

People are generally cynical about making suggestions to policymakers, assuming that no one reads them. In my earlier book (Your Vote is Not Enough), towards the end, I have appended twelve letters/emails received from Chief Ministers, Union Minister, Prime Minister's office, to make a point on how the politicians and officials take action on suggestions. People think it is tough to analyse, and it is too 'technical'. Actually it is not like that. If you cannot handle it alone, find or form a group of likeminded friends who are passionate about an issue and then, start analysing the surroundings and start questioning the local office for its failure – whether it is a blocked drain, erratic electric supply or a bad road. You have paid your taxes every time you paid GST while buying something, in addition to the income tax. Every Indian, even the beggars or destitute, pay the taxes, and so, it is our right to hold officers and leaders accountable for using this tax money. RTI is a useful tool to get information.

Officers or public servants are obliged to deliver what they have been appointed for without being arrogant or/and ignorant. India fails as we let her down by being a silent spectator. Our right to question is our undisputable right, and it is something we don't use and so, we fail India every time something goes wrong and we wait for someone else to do our job. Take your responsibility of bringing the first change. Hold people accountable. So, Observe – Read – Think – Analyse – Take Action. If you are not driving accountability at the bottom, why are you expecting it from the top! Governance is not a top-down process, it is always driven bottom-up. If we fail in our duty, it sets a chain reaction for failure at every level, starting with 'us'!

Officers have to serve and not Govern. We must deliver what is expected of us.

No matter who we are – be it a sanitation worker, teacher, doctor, engineer, bureaucrat, or a political leader – at our level, we have to deliver on our roles without fear or favour. I have served the government, and I had joined the government for my passion to be a part of the system to bring about a change in policies for my country. Having been a part of the system for over three years, I did not take any salary, and serving as an advisor to the Union Minister, I chose to not even take allowances. I had chosen to accept the offer and serve the government and not let government serve me. It was my duty and not my entitlement. In every role, as long as I thought I was making a meaningful contribution, I stayed and post that, I quit to contribute towards more meaningful endeavours. While serving as an advisor to a Union Minister, I was asked many times that I should renovate my office and change the computer, printer, and air conditioner as they were old. I declined the offer as I considered it a wasteful expense and just requested for the chairs to be cleaned. After duty hours, I travelled by Metro or walked to the meetings. Even, as a member of a central government-appointed commission, I was entitled to car and a protocol officer of the rank of an additional director, but I chose to decline the services of the protocol officer, as I considered that the officers must be in their offices doing their duty and not following me like a shadow and demeaning their role and responsibility. When once, a protocol officer insisted that he would be at the airport to receive me, I had to send him a message, 'Please do not come to the airport, I will take a cab and come to office'. Officer then asked me, 'Who will receive you at the office when you arrive'. I had to tell him, 'As a commission member, I have the office address, and I will have no problem finding the venue for the meeting. Please go ahead and attend to your duty in office'. I easily used the cab sharing service and reached the meeting. It actually costed me 15–20% of what the government would have spent on my travels. Entitled to Hotel Janpath in Delhi, I stayed in a government hostel next door at a much cheaper accommodation. Entitled to business class travel, I declined, as in an LMIC country, it would be a wasteful expense to travel business class for frequent meetings. Also, serving as an advisor to a Union Minister, I spent personal money for all my travel, stay in Delhi and serving refreshments to visitors at my office. I was told that, as an advisor to the Minister, I have unrestricted access to refreshments from his canteen, but I always avoided it. So, I was always conscious of the fact that, I was here to serve.

Those who have visited bureaucrats will find that every officer, no matter which level one is, will have a TV and set top box in the office, and while someone is talking, one eye will be glued to the news on the TV, while they 'hear' you, giving an impression that, the officers are not actually 'listening', but 'pretending to listen', and they quickly wish to dispose off the visitor. Why should officers have a TV with a set-top box when they have all the newspapers and magazines subscribed at taxpayers' expense? I have interacted with dozens of people in the Government and other organizations who matter to this country. I am giving an example of just four people at the top who have made an impact on my work.

The personality which impressed me with his focus is Dr. Mohan Bhagwat. If he is in a meeting, there is no TV in the room, no mobile and no other paper on his desk. He is all ears and focused on the discussion. Something I wouldn't have expected of such a senior and busy personality.

Once I met the Prime Minister in his parliament office the very next day the GST was passed in parliament, and you can imagine how busy and thoughtful the PM might have been, given the historical development of the passage of GST, and the parliament in session at the time. The first thing he did before our meeting started was to mute the TV and focus on our discussion. Imagine – he is the PM of our country, and I am of no consequence as a party worker. But he was in full attention.

Shri. Amit Shah is another politician who is informal and has no distraction during the meeting. He is focussed on what is being talked about and is very particular on facts and figures.

Shri. J.P Nadda has a unique quality – give him two pages to read, and in the time he glances through it, he has grasped everything. If you get 20 minutes from him, it is worth one hour from any other politician.

Why did I give an example of these four top people? Even at their positions, they will never lose attention and focus in the meetings, but, even a joint secretary-level officer will be lost on the phone or will be busy with his computer or television. This culture needs to change. We must remove TV from all offices, and the officials should become professional in their dealings.

Also, such officers who end up spending money in beautifying their offices and having multiple printers and cold-water and hot-water dispensers and spending the major chunk of the budgets during the fag end of the quarter in hosting meetings in five-star hotels to spend the budget allocations, don't deserve to be in office. I have witnessed multiple scenarios in the government. I am convinced to conclude that every officer of the government must be careful not to squander away the poor country's tax payer's money for beautifying their office or leading a luxurious life, forgetting that tens of millions suffer from malnourishment and poverty and don't even have the basics of life.

Bureaucrats are strictly hierarchy driven and have multiple times the ego than the knowledge about their office or subject they are handling, and this lets them get away with their rudeness. If you are an officer who practices the things written above, you don't work for India, you work for yourself, and still if you consider such things as an entitlement, it is indicative of your moral turpitude and lack of ethics. It is time to fix such issues as a step towards a culture of serving and not governing. Also, bureaucrats and judges should not be appointed to any position post-retirement or given extension under any circumstances.

Politicians are also at fault for not doing their job well. Even in the Modi Government, 80 percent, if not more ministers, are living off the popularity of the Prime Minister and bidding time making statements that are uncalled for, and not delivering on their primary role. I think it is time that people started voting for qualifications and expertise to hold such public offices.

Also, it might be worthwhile for a CSO (Civil Society Organization) to develop an Artificial Intelligence (AI) based software that tracks all the speeches, promises, actions, and cases against public figures. Such a tech-driven solution may help decide which person can fit a role to deliver in office, and such informed choices from the electorate may drastically alter the course of politics. Such a solution might be a little away, but till then, citizens must hold their chosen leaders accountable to their promises and actions. The culture of politicians with criminal cases and money bags must end, and those with knowledge and passion must join politics for the transformation of India. This is a crucial step, and without educated politicians, bureaucrats will have a field day and will continue to ravage the nation without accountability. Again, this change has to be driven by ground-level leaders of change, i.e. you. For this, we need a mindset change!

'Mindset change is the toughest. But if we change our mindsets, the next thing that should happen is a systemic change. Without changing our mindsets, we should not expect any lasting systemic changes, the real change'.

Systemic Change

Though systemic changes are tough, as the current system serves well for everyone from top to bottom, which is based on 'Give and Take' or 'Get as you Pay', not only it can be managed, the beneficiaries can manipulate it as well! If ever there was a fair assessment for the amount of wealth India lost due to corruption and inefficiency of bureaucracy, it would far exceed the amount Britishers ripped us off in over 190 years they ruled India. While the British ripped India neatly of its wealth and culture through their imperial bureaucracy, they built infrastructure like railways, post offices, police, and judiciary with our money as well. We have lost much more since Independence through the same system (bureaucratic system) they created for ripping off India, and we happily let their same system ruin us unabated.

For changing the system, we have to understand and prioritise, which systemic changes will have the most impact. To my understanding, Judiciary and Police come at the top and then the administrative and then, electoral reforms. Without undertaking any of these reforms, any talk of making India a developed country will just amount to kite flying or remain a pipe dream. The first thing to address is judicial reforms.

Judicial & Police Reforms

For India to become a developed nation with safe and happy citizens, it needs to ensure the safety of people with time-bound delivery of justice and enforcement of the law.

The perception for Indian police and judiciary is that, they are not only incompetent and inefficient but also insufficient. Here, just a mere filling of the vacancies will not help, as also, the way they are filled. In fact, under the current setup, increasing the number of personnel in the judiciary and police will lead to building upon the legacy issues and will further deepen the malaise. Judiciary and the police need major reforms. Every political party has promised it, but finally, they also feel helpless to transform the judiciary and police for various reasons. It is time to take bold decisions. Finally, it is the legislature that is accountable to people and represents the will of the people and has its mandate, so it must ensure that reforms are done as per the wishes of the people and the needs of our time. It must be its highest priority and responsibility to transform judiciary and police and make it accountable and outcome-driven to become a key enabler for New India.

Appointment & Promotion System

Judges should not appoint judges and neither should it be dependent on political leadership. We have enough examples in the highest court, where fingers have been pointed on crucial decisions in the past. Appointment of judges from the lowest level to the highest level should be driven by a transparent competency assessment. Thereafter, all promotions should follow the standard evaluation for professionalism and efficiency. The Government or the judges should not be involved in appointments, and this is important for the judiciary to maintain fairness and independence.

Also, in India, the judgments are delivered over generations and ages and not in weeks or months. Punishment for defaults and crimes are financial and in the form of imprisonment which lack effective enforcement, and there are enough loopholes in the system to circumvent it, so the crime graph has not come down. Instead the crimes are committed with impunity. Judiciary has become a refuge of unscrupulous elements and torture for the victims. Judiciary needs to change.

1. Filling up vacancies and promotions: we can make the delivery of justice time-bound and all promotions in police and judiciary should not be based on age or seniority, but only on professional contribution and efficiency. The judge who delivers maximum judgments per year and whose judgments are not changed or reversed by other courts should be elevated in a comparative assessment of the bench/courts. Objective performance evaluation should be the sole criteria for a periodic evaluation of the judges or justices of a court, irrespective of the number of years in service in a particular year/ bench. Also, steps must be taken to ensure that there is no 'ganging up by judges to go slow on judgments. When this is implemented, we will see fast track judgments. Also, for a crime, the SOP (standard operating procedure) or guidelines with time frames must be adhered to from the court and the complainant's side.

Evidence does not get created, and arguments are not a time-bound biological process. So, the judgements cannot be dragged for decades. There must be a comprehensive study to put a time frame to delivery of justice, and digital tools must be used to avoid repeat adjournment of court hearings and also, to ensure the privacy of hearings.

2. A proper system of checks and balances is needed. Else, we will keep loading the court with cases and adjournments, emboldening the might of the criminals and anti-social elements. We must remove the black ribbon from the eyes of the judiciary and let it keep its eyes wide open to the changing realities of our time.

3. Monetary fines for defaults should be exemplary. It will serve twin purpose; a) Huge financial outflow will in itself become a deterrent for defaulters b) It will make the judiciary and police sustainable. Take, for example, in August 2018, there was an uproar on how old UIDAI helpline numbers got into the phone address book of Indians (Khan D., 2018). Well, today it was the old helpline number finding its way into the phone address book, but it could very well have been a criminal's number or a number of any anti-social element, to defame and tarnish the reputation of an honest and an upright individual. Question is how, and why did google

do it in the first place? Who gave it the authority, and even if it did this, why did it go unnoticed? So, ultimately no one was held accountable for this serious breach. Maybe, Google should have been made to pay 5% of its global revenues as fine, and Indian lawmakers should have grilled its CEO. This serious privacy breach became a piece of big news for a few days, and then, all was over. Are we a banana republic that foreign entities can mess around and getaway? Can this happen in the US? India should learn and implement strict enforcement.

4. Similarly, in the police, promotions should be based on the number of cases registered and solved & how the public rates the police official who served them.

5. People are lodged in jails for crimes, and on taxpayer's money!! This must change, and criminals must pay for their stay without any subsidy. The financial fines should cover for their stay in jails, or those who cannot afford to pay fine must work extra to make up for the cost of their stay, unless they are medically unfit.

6. Police should be trained for soft skills, and if they fail to solve less than 80% of the cases, they should be transferred or demoted.

All these initiatives will also mean filling lakhs of vacancies in the judiciary and police and making it self-sustainable and not dependent on government funds. The most common excuse is that the government doesn't have the resources to fund recruitment, and hence there are vacancies in the judiciary and law enforcement. This will not be an argument anymore if we change the meagre amount we charge as fines and start charging exemplary fines. Most importantly, people will regain trust in the most important arm of the government. Also, crime and illegal practices will come down drastically due to time-bound delivery of justice. Finally, it will lead to India becoming more obedient and compliant with laws. This will also make us more productive when we avoid wasting our time in courts and court cases, which will help us move ahead on our journey to become a developed nation.

Governance Reforms

It is futile to address any issue without addressing the bedrocks of governance and administration – public representatives, and equally pointless to expect any worthwhile change in the country without reforming the governance. This has to be the overarching theme if we are aiming at making India a developed country.

Members of Parliament (MPs): We are still following the system of parliamentary representation with 550 MPs, based on the 1970 census, when the population of India was 54.8 crores. Then, almost half a century ago, each MP represented a population of 10 lakhs in parliament, and today, when the population has more than doubled, the average population served by an MP is about 24 lakhs. How can a single MP serve 24 lakh people? Is it not time to reconsider the number of seats in parliament so that the population per MP is manageable? The fact remains that any readjustment in the number of constituencies cannot be undertaken until 2026, in keeping with the Constitution (Amendment) Act 2002, but are we being fair to our MPs, or to the people they represent?

It is also urgent that the parameters on which an MP can be independently and transparently assessed be defined, and they be trained in policy and execution. With these measures in place, the MPs, the real lawmakers of the country, will deliver for which the electorate sends them to the parliament. The issue of creating and maintaining clear indicators becomes even more important because even though the quality of ministers is majorly decided by the 'electorate' through the Lok Sabha, key portfolios are being held by MPs from the Rajya Sabha.

Each minister should ideally present a performance scorecard which should include, among others: new initiatives taken, delivery of programs through the number of lives touched—including, but not limited to, actual fund utilization for beneficiaries (as part of the funds are absorbed in travel, administration, and office infrastructure), resolution of grievances, surprise visits undertaken, and action taken against non-performers and corrupt officials. We can keep adding parameters, but the critical point is to ensure that ministers are not mere figureheads who blindly sign documents presented to them by bureaucrats.

Today, bureaucrats prevail upon ministers in almost everything; but if the ministers knew their subject well and did their homework, bureaucratic logjams and red-tape could be reduced, and the country could fast-track development. Most of the ministers of state have no direct responsibility except laying papers in the parliament and cutting ribbons at inaugurations. If this does not change, we will be wasting precious resources. Finally, the public should start rating the performance of ministries and ministers. If citizens' lives are touched and the work accomplished is visible on the ground, it is the public that is in the best position to decide who performed and how, and who failed to deliver. This public rating should be institutionalized for every minister, ministry and government office, and must be run transparently by an independent agency digitally.

In line with expectation of good performance from an MP, the MP must be provided with enough support staff and budgets. This will ensure that the MP can serve the people of his constituency, and not seek help from business houses for support staff for which they have to oblige the business houses, and in-turn compromise with their legislative oath, professional independence, integrity, and obligations.

The Convergence of Departments: Some of the ministries and departments should be merged because we currently have a strange system that operates in silos.

Here are a few classic examples: Nutrition (under the ICDS scheme) is under the Ministry of Women and Child Development; pharmaceuticals and medical devices are under the Ministry of Chemicals and Fertilizers, while other aspects related to health are looked after by the Ministry of Health and Family Welfare. Employee State Insurance Corporation (ESIC) Hospitals come under the Ministry of Labour, while the Ex-Servicemen Contributory Health Scheme (ECHS) comes under the Ministry of Defence. There are at least twenty-six ministries that handle matters related to health.

The Ministry of Human Resource Development, the Ministry of Culture, and the Ministry of Skill Development and Entrepreneurship are three different ministries. Isn't the mandate of MHRD also the development of skills and the promotion of culture? Would it not make more sense to include entrepreneurship under the Ministry of Micro, Small and Medium Enterprises?

How can rural development happen without agriculture? Should not the ministries of Agriculture and Rural Development be merged? This merger could seed the overarching dream of the development of rural India, with a focus on agriculture.

What would make the most sense is to converge ministries with a broader mandate under a single cabinet minister, adding more ministers of state. They would shoulder the responsibility, along with their cabinet colleague, of creating and achieving a broader vision for the country in that particular sector. Without these convergences, there is bound to be infighting, and work that happens in independent silos. These will prevent things from happening, and the country will suffer from slow growth.

Finally, political parties must realise that political realignment or horse-trading for winning elections and coming to power will take India backward, and the youth of the country is growing impatient with such a system. Also, such leaders are not making any positive difference to India's development. We need educated people with deep expertise to fight elections and transform India into a developed nation. Every major political party must address this issue.

Administrative Reforms

Bureaucracy has been the biggest bottleneck for India's progress. In as much as people blame politicians, but the fact remains, that when 'bureaucracy' is called the 'perpetual government', can we put the entire blame on politicians who come and go every five years? There are exceptions of great bureaucrats, but far and few in between.

We cannot run a 21st-century government with an administrative structure which was designed for the 18th century. India has suffered immensely from its outdated administrative setup and poor governance, which results from it. In reality, the whole system is crumbling and regressive. This situation has not changed even in the last few years, despite a technocratic and bold Prime Minister at the helm. If we are aiming to transform governance and the administration, we must be sure of one thing: the bureaucracy will resist all measures which will bring in transparency and accountability, as bureaucrats love authority but hate accountability. Moreover, if we entrust the bureaucracy with correcting itself, no major change will ever happen. Therefore, it is the Prime Minister himself who will have to find a 'close team' that can deliver this as a reform. If major bureaucratic reforms are carried out, they will need a nod from Parliament. They will be sufficient to demonstrate the commitment of the government as well as the maturity of our lawmakers. Without these, there can be no meaningful change in India. Once these plans of reform are formulated, we need speed, efficiency, and effectiveness in our entire chain of command to implement them.

The primary goal of the reform is *'a system in which interfacing with the government will not mean interference on its part; where communications with the government will not take on the tone of insults, and getting work done in the government will not become harassment'*. We need a complete overhaul in the system, a shift in culture and mindset, which will change the bureaucracy from its administrative role to a service-oriented one, where they serve citizens, making life more convenient for us and enhancing our prosperity. It calls for a massive cultural change, along with changes in systems of delivery and performance evaluation. We must remember that, while accountability can be tracked with systems, it must be enforced with the relevant work culture. Without a genuine change in culture and mindset, people will find a way to circumvent any system, checkmate it, and make it dysfunctional.

The reforms in our bureaucracy are crucial to make it more effective, and to bring it in tune with the needs of the time. Of course, all these reforms will take time, but we can start with fixing clearly defined goals and deliverables for every government employee with immediate effect

There are three kinds of 'corruption' in bureaucracy: one is of pay and gets it done; second, is the inordinate delay in routine issues, and file movement becomes like a biological process and leads to cost overrun. Sadly, more the file moves back and forth, the more hardworking a bureaucrat is considered. The third kind of corruption is, of not taking a decision and not being accountable to anyone. This is based on the belief that there is no punishment for not making a decision. You can only be caught if you make a decision. This needs to change, and reforms include, amongst others;

1. Fixing clear deliverables for every officer in the government. This will also lead to deciding fixed tenures, and reasons for such postings and mid-term transfers, which must be put in the public domain. Of all the reforms, this is the one that can happen immediately. The rest will involve a lot of procedures.

2. Assessment and evaluation against the deliverables, including rating by the public whom they have dealt during the appraisal period.

3. End of tenured service for the Joint Secretary and above.

4. Restricting the file movement to three levels and a time frame to clear files at each level.

5. Allowing individual responsibility rather than forming committees.

6. Lateral entry of subject matter experts in place of civil servants.

7. Revolving door policy between academia, industry and civil service.

8. Generalized cadre being dissolved and replaced with domain experts under provincial and national level civil service.

9. Salary and rewards for civil services be at par with the best in the world.

10. Non-performance be dealt strictly, leading to a demotion for the first lapse, and lateral exit during the subsequent lapse.

11. Performance evaluation of every bureaucrat be put in public domain.

12. If an officer is transferred mid-term, then the reason for such a transfer has to be explained in

writing, and the same posted in public domain by the officer ordering transfer.

13. CSS (Central Civil Services) rule book needs to be rewritten with the changing needs of time.

Reforming Bureaucracy

- The current performance appraisal system of Annual Confidential Reports (ACRs) have now become meaningless. Since ACRs are written by bureaucrats – for bureaucrats, the norm is 'do no harm'. People are generally rated between 8–10 in their ACRs, and the pattern continues year after year, batch after batch.

- The present-day approach of bureaucrats is to 'control' and 'govern' and not to, 'work as a team' for 'development'. Also, most officials work in silos, and for themselves, governed by their egos and, at times, petty impulses, which may pit one official against the other. With this attitude, there can never be a team approach in whatever they do.

- Bureaucrats are more 'procedure driven' than 'outcome driven', which is why files routinely take months to travel from one desk to another. If we expect major improvements in delivery with such an approach, they will not happen. The bureaucracy must be service oriented, accountable and outcome driven.

Therefore, we need the following major changes:

- The first major transformation is that the entrance examination for civil services should be phased out and only specialists who have the relevant degree of knowledge or work experience in a particular department should be inducted into it. For example, a primary school teacher, based on his/her qualification, experience and outstanding achievements, should have an opportunity at becoming Secretary, Education. In the same way, a nurse, health worker, physiotherapist, pharmacist or a doctor, should have a chance at running a district health administration and even becoming the Secretary, Health. If the departments of Defence and Science and Technology have never depended on the Indian Administrative Services to run them, and delivered good results, why are we running other departments with officers with no domain expertise?

- All serving employees of the government must have clearly defined weekly routine, monthly, quarterly and yearly deliverables and targets. If they fail to deliver three times in a row, they must be demoted and if they become repeat offenders, their services must be terminated.

- Lateral entry and lateral exit should be made an integral part of the administrative (bureaucratic) system.

- The training pattern of bureaucrats, and the Central Civil Services (CCS) rules must be modified to reflect the needs of an LMIC country transitioning into a developing country.

- All public officers must get feedback and ratings from actual users, with details.

- Every official must disclose the direct cost to the government, which includes the cost of his office, including his dedicated staff, trainings in India and abroad, so that the public knows how much money is being spent by the government on an official to serve the public.

- As of now, we have an appraisal system that looks at ACRs, which only factors an individual's performance. We must move from the ACR system to the CPR (Comprehensive Performance Review) system.

- Foreign trainings make no sense. When the bureaucrats are serving Indian population, they should be trained in India. It is a blot on our system that we spend crores of rupees on training a babu abroad to serve villages in India !!

Comprehensive Performance Review System

- An Individual Performance Review (IPR), which should be based on quarterly and yearly goals or assigned deliverables, to be decided by the head of the department. This chain should be followed, down the line, for every government employee, whether permanent or contractual. Soft skills, especially in the handling of the public, must be an integral part of the training, and a key criterion in the assessment of performance. The following weightages within the IPR will ensure even closer attention to detail:

1. Defining time-bound quantifiable and measurable deliverables (15 per cent).

2. Completion of targets within the proposed time frame (15 per cent).

3. Completion of targets without increase in budgets (15 per cent).

4. Utilization of funds (15 per cent).

5. Disposal of files and grievances (10 per cent).

6. Innovations (15 per cent).

7. Customer service feedback from the citizens (public) who interfaced with the officer (15 per cent).

8. The weightage should be objectively apportioned for any misses in achieving targets.

- An annual Department Performance Review (DPR), in which an assessment of a department's performance is evaluated, based on the goals set for the quarter/year. This review should also include a service and delivery feedback mechanism to assess if citizens are being treated with respect or are being ill handled. The individual weightages for the DPR could be as follows:

1. Identifying key annual deliverables and priorities, to be done by the minister in-charge and officers up to the rank of Joint Secretary (15 per cent).

2. The completion of pre-set targets within the time frame (15 per cent).

3. The achievement of targets without an increase in budgets (15 per cent).

4. Full, and judicious utilization of funds (15 per cent).

5. The disposal of grievances (15 per cent).

6. Feedback from the people who interfaced with the department for work (25 per cent).

- A Government Performance Review (GPR), which is an overall performance rating of the Government based on feedback from a public survey taken from citizens for all the departments and ministries, whether in the district, the states, or at the Centre, where one has interfaced. All the metrics which form the basis of performance must be based on actual verifiable data. The following weightages are key to assess performance:

1. The implementation of key announcements versus the goals achieved in terms of beneficiaries or actual lives touched (10 per cent).

2. Ensuring that inflation targets are met, and the prices of essential household. consumable products controlled (10 per cent).

3. Keeping the fiscal deficit under control (10 per cent).

4. Ensuring the development and growth of the country (10 per cent).

5. The utilization of funds and achieving an increase in the number of beneficiaries of schemes (10 per cent).

6. Achieving a reduction in poverty (10 per cent).

7. Increase in GDP per capita or an alternative indicator (10 per cent).

8. The disposal of grievances (10 per cent).

9. As with any other provider of services, feedback from the ultimate consumers is crucial. The government must work for public welfare, and if the work done by the government is visible on the ground and felt by the public, it must

also be judged by the public. Hence, genuine feedback should have a weightage of 20 per cent. This feedback can be made via Interactive Voice Response (IVR) system, or some other suitable mechanism so that it is not misused.

- To calculate the overall CPR of individual officers, the IPR should be allocated 40 per cent; the DPR 30 per cent and the GPR 30 per cent.

- The CPR can be implemented from the level of the Secretary and moved downwards in a phased manner in the next five years. Till this reform on performance is done, bureaucrats will remain in 'sleep mode', as their retirement age is fixed and they, in a real sense, don't bother about the government of the day or its vision or programs.

- It goes without saying that the CPR should not have any reservation or weightage for any category and be based strictly on merit and performance that have been transparently and objectively assessed.

- This public rating should be run transparently by an independent agency and only through digital medium & the user should be verified, but anonymous, for getting an honest feedback and to rule out any scope for victimization of honest reviewers.

Modifying the Tenured System

While job security is a wonderful thing, and enshrined within the terms of employment, it is also the biggest bane of bureaucracy. We must modify the system, keeping job security centre stage, but only for those officers who have performed well, and have been judged through a transparent appraisal system. If the Government is serious about a 'Big Change', the second major reform after judiciary/police is bureaucracy and the rest will fall in place.

All officers of head of department rank (starting from district magistrates) must be put on a five-year contract term, based on a review of their performance, with decent financial incentives and award for outstanding work. On the other hand, if they fail to live up to a minimum IPR of 80 per cent for three years out of a five-year term, they must be relieved from service. Good performance should be the sole criteria to decide seniority, despite the fact that the term of employment is contractual. All pay hikes and promotions should be based on the CPR and the financial incentives for good performance should be at par with the best in any other sector and should add to their service record.

As a corollary, no official or minister should be allowed to travel business class or undergo any training abroad. This is sheer wastage of public money, which can otherwise be used for productive investment.

Also, for every middle – and senior-level position, there should be a clearly defined succession plan.

The officer-designate should chip in as and when needed, so that delivery of services is not affected. Also, no bureaucrat should be given any extension or post-retirement assignment.

eOffice and eFile Systems: No file pertaining to government work should pass more than three levels, and each level should not take more than a week. If more information is required for a decision, or more time is needed, this needs to be noted on the file with a proper justification. Moving the file system online will allow officials more mobility, since they can access them from either handheld devices, or laptops. This will free them up, so that 20–30 per cent of their time is spent in the field, meeting and interacting with the people whom they serve. Moving the decision-making process online will have another significant impact – It will curtail verbal orders and decision-making. No verbal instructions should be allowed at any level; they can only be issued online, through eOffice and eFile.

The biggest challenge in changing the system is that this 'fiefdom ' is iron-walled by the same bureaucrats who will have to change it, and so, it will need a strong outsider at the top with a few chosen bureaucrats in DOPT (Department of Personnel and Training, which comes under the PMO) to bring about the change. The bureaucrats may be resistant to such a reform, but it is the will and commitment from the political leadership which can make this happen.

Electoral Reforms

We need people who are educated and come with a clean record and are not backed by lobbies, criminals, or vested interests. Despite having electoral reforms, things haven't changed. We can routinely read criminal acts by public representatives – from being involved in financial frauds to heinous rape crimes. This calls for a major change.

Funding of political parties: Only those who vote should contribute to election funds. So, corporate funding should stop. To me, corporate funding of political parties is like an 'advance bribe' for seeking post-victory favours. This distorts the entire policy making and governance. Why should those who don't vote, give funds to a political party ? Well, if they would give a logic that they believe in the ideology and would support the government, then they should use their CSR (Corporate Social Responsibility) funds or directly contribute to the Prime Minister's or the Chief Minister's fund of their respective states, or whichever state they wish to support. Else, corporate funding of elections is like a *quid pro quo*. Also, minimum, a graduate qualification should be made must for public representatives if India has to become a developed nation. As mentioned above, CSOs (Civil Society Organizations) could develop an AI backed tool about public figures and predict their performance based on prior track record. This could bring a major change in the way political parties choose candidates and electorates vote for a candidate.

Data

'We have three problems when it comes to the availability of data; integrity, integration and intelligence'

Data is our weakest link as far as policy making or analysis are concerned. In conducting research for this book, I could not find a go-to source which would provide me data on India. E.g. the number of jobs, the number of loans disbursed to individuals or to industries, the number of people in the middle class, the number of farmers, the number of retailers, among others. How can one plan for the country in the absence of data and based only on census figures from 2011, which is a decade old? The government must leverage the Digital India programme to ensure that population wise and sectoral data are available and updated live. This is one of the biggest drawbacks in planning—that data is not available, and if available, it is old and patchy and full of discrepancies. A website was launched by the government, https://data.gov.in/, but the data for key indicators is census based and dates back to 2011, which is of little use for drafting policies for today. If India has to move towards evidence based policy making, it is important that we move towards a system where the population census data is not more than three years. Anything older than that is of no consequence in policy making. For most of the programs and projects, ideally, the data should be live in this digital age.

Rules and Regulations

All rules and regulations must be simple, unambiguous, and easy to understand. This will go a long way in taking away the largely arbitrary power of discretion from the administrative machinery, which must only be entrusted with execution and service delivery, on behalf of the government. Ideally, no government policy document should be more than fifteen pages long and no form should be more than two pages. Rules and regulations must be system driven, so that they do not need committees to ponder over and ratify them. For instance, all increases in income and taxes should be linked to inflation data, with a predefined formula. Also, all rules must be reviewed and changed with time, ideally, every decade.

All government departments should have a digital dashboard which indicates how many beneficiaries connected with them per month. Similarly, every scheme of the government must have a digital dashboard, updated live, which will show the number of beneficiaries, funds allocated, funds disbursed and funds utilized.

Most importantly, artificial barriers are uncalled for in today's age and need to be done away with. These barriers include; demands such as asking for bank drafts that are issued only by nationalized banks, affidavits which must be attested by notaries, documents which need to be attested – either by gazetted officers or other authorities, demands made for proofs of identity and residence, among others. We must trust and respect our citizens. E.g. Since PAN and AADHAR are linked, which form the basis of KYC (Know Your Customer) for any bank account and other services, so, if KYC has been done for one service, automatically all the PAN/AADHAR linked account and services should be KYC verified. If needed, a centralized KYC registry may be created. Why is a person required to go to all the bank and service providers for the same, wasting papers in photo-copying and moreover, time, which is in fact killing all the productivity? We must build our systems in such a way that there are inbuilt checks and balances, and information is not only readily available, but also private and protected. The removal of these artificial barriers will not only make the lives of citizens easier, but also boost productivity.

The governments, both at the Centre and the States, should create unified portals along the lines of www.publicopinion.gov.in or www.opinion.gov.in, so that people will not have to wade through multiple government websites to figure out which document or issue is put in public domain for comments and suggestions. This will ensure that people become active participants in governance by sharing their views on important topics, government bills, acts and documents. Also, the best and the brightest ideas received from the public should be recognized, so that people are motivated to participate in the processes of policy making and reform.

Education

*'Education is the cause of economic development
and not the result of it'.*

This is the fundamental thing that people have to understand. As we pass through COVID-19, we have seen that only a handful of scientists and institutions could gear up for creating testing kits or work towards vaccines which the world needs to fight COVID-19. This is when, we have states in India which are comparable to many countries across the world in terms of population. This is a wake-up call and a call to action to redo our education policy and create an education system which prepares India to take care of its population, and prepares it for unexpected exigencies like; COVID-19, skirmishes, or even wars from hostile neighbours, besides providing us the best in the world human resources, which will help us build and run world class enterprises. Sadly, we teach even science as history, so how will the students become futuristic? Let us understand that, 'Education for All' does not mean 'Same Education for All'. So, it needs careful planning with regards to primary, secondary and tertiary education and research for making India a developed nation. A government which is not serious about education and health, cannot be serious about development.

Everyone is talking about the 'Economy Post-COVID', and equally important discussion should be about 'Education Post-COVID', and this needs an immediate action plan. Every aspect of the transformation of education is covered in detail in my previous book 'Your Degree is Not Enough', along with a prescriptive 'Education Policy for GenNext', which details out the actions needed, along with defined goals.

It is high time that we work on transforming education in parallel with other reforms and investments.

Healthcare

'Poverty leads to disease, and disease leads to poverty. Disease and Poverty are good friends and stay together'

Twenty three years ago, on this day, my mother passed away battling an advanced stage cancer. The moment she died, we became below poverty line within minutes from APL (Above Poverty Line). We had her dead body, but no money to do her last rites, as we had spent all the money in her treatment. My mother was a class one government employee. So, I have seen how diseases can lead to economic turmoil.

Now, COVID-19 has shown everyone across the world that, it is not the economic muscle or the military power which decides a super-power, and that, the economic power without a robust healthcare system, can bring the economic super-power to its knees. Imagine the world's mightiest nations struggling for PPE or HCQ supplies and pleading, threatening and offering monetary baits to get such supplies, and still, as we pass through COVID-19, no one knows what the new world order would be, once this gets over. This has brought the focus back to healthcare system, and given a strong message that, *India needs to be a healthcare super-power, before becoming an economic super-power.*

In 2014, when I was drafting the Election Manifesto of the BJP, I utilized the opportunity to write the first point in the healthcare section as drafting a National Healthcare Policy on priority, and I was also involved in drafting of the National Health Policy 2017. This has clearly identifiable goals and key action points. We have a choice to go the public healthcare route or take to privatized healthcare which is essentially a sick-care path. Since I have written extensively on healthcare and the way forward in my book, 'Healthcare Reforms in India – Making up for the Lost Decades', I will not go in complete details here, but just mention a few pointers. The key policy directions are mentioned in the National Health Policy 2017, as approved by the Government. The following pointers should be considered;

- We have to strengthen the public healthcare system.

- Adopt the pre-emptive care model – focusing on child health. We need to build a healthcare system which pre-empts the occurrence of diseases in children and youth and also takes care of chronic diseases.

- Adopt digital tools – extensively.

- Strategic purchasing from private sector as a short-term measure is to ensure that poor people don't die for want of care which is not currently available with the public sector.

- In the interim, we must strengthen the public sector with adequate focus on prevention.

- We need to create a special cadre of healthcare workers for senior citizens, and ramp up our network of senior citizen communities and hospices.

- We will have to create a hospital-based 'hub and spoke model', which is fully integrated to take care of people at the first level of getting into the healthcare system. This healthcare model has not to be doctor and allopathic centric, but may be driven by paramedics, and AYUSH.

- We should extensively use technology for fitness and nutrition as an overarching theme.

- We need to come out with activity-based guidelines and calorie exchange, to help people choose the fitness regimen and the right diet.

- Set up 'Health Helpline' in all major Indian languages for teleconsultation with ePrescription.

- This system should be publicly administered and centrally delivered with a limited role for private players, based on 'pay for outcomes'.

- Public health and public sector should never be undermined in healthcare delivery of the nation. National Health Policy 2017 (Ministry of Health & Family Welfare, Government of India, 2020) is quite an exhaustive document with a clear direction, and if implemented, we will be on the right path toward making a 'Healthy India'.

Integrated Transport and Logistics

'Speed, Safety, Savings, and Productivity'

Just building roads, transit systems, waterways, and airports should not be the goal. Why do we build them and what do these transport and logistics system deliver to the nation and its citizens? The sole criteria should be – Speed, Safety, Savings, and Productivity.

The overarching theme should be integration of transport services with an 'India Travel Card'. This card should be good to use across road, rail and waterways.

Also, it is seen that there is a mad rush to start metro trains in many small towns which normally can be traversed in 30–40 minutes with wider roads and traffic management. Such towns should not invest in metros. Not only that it is a much bigger hassle than widening the road, with metros being created, passenger transport in such towns through other modes will drastically reduce, resulting in job losses. So, if the metro has to be built, a proper justification (through feasibility study) should be done with regards to cost of building, maintenance cost, travel cost, paying capacity of the population, and net job creation (factoring job losses). Ideally, we must hold these projects till India reaches the middle income country status and then, have a fresh look at all metro or bullet train proposals. With COVID-19, we have to rationalise our capital investment. The thumb rule is, any capital investment we do, must lead to a cascading effect in terms of creating more business and employment opportunities, besides meeting its objective of making the lives of citizens hassle free and easier.

Despite paying toll taxes, in addition to road taxes, upfront, the roads – even in the financial capital, Mumbai, are in a bad shape, and this is despite them being repaired every year. Time has come to lay stringent norms for contractors who take up such projects. If the company fails to adhere to building quality roads, financial fines should be made stringent, with jail terms for the company owners and the superintending engineer of the project and the public representative (ward representative and MLA) of that area.

Also, it is seen that the speed-breakers are not marked and are of varying heights in different places. There needs to be uniformity in speed-breakers specifications, along with proper marking and signs on the road about the speed-breaker ahead. Not only this is the cause of vehicle damage, but also accidents, leading to serious injury and deaths.

Also, heavy vehicles (which are driven slower than passenger vehicles) should be provided with a designated lane and this must be enforced with strict norms. Not only this will increase movement speed, but also cut down accidents.

Toll must be abolished as every Indian is paying multiple taxes like GST, road tax, registration tax on vehicles and even taking insurance, which isn't cheap by any standards. Time to overhaul the transport and logistics network across the country to boost productivity.

Soft Infrastructure

During COVID-19, the world changed, hard infrastructure was not used by more than 95% of the population or may be 99% of the population, but internet and cellular services were used by one and all. Whether you are a student, businessperson or a professional, every one of us realised the importance of soft infrastructure in such a crisis.

India is planning for launching 5G. But even our 3G and 4G don't work properly. Sometimes people switch to data calls or use WIFI at home to make calls over data. This is pathetic! And moreover, the telecom companies are under severe financial stress. Once, India had about a dozen telecom providers, and now, we are left with only three private players and a government player, and of them, three are in a bad financial shape. This financial condition of the telecom sector is due to faulty policies regarding the airwaves auctions, which are a sovereign asset. Why should the government sell airwaves? By selling airwaves, the government filled its coffers collecting lakhs of crores of rupees, but the problem remained as such. Telecom companies took lakhs of crore loans from the banks, and with losses reeling, these loans will turn into NPAs, or those investors who invested with the hope of high returns in telecom sector would have now billed losses or written off their investments. Moreover, telecom, which should have become enabler for digital India, has become more of a liability. Not a single citizen of this country can claim a seamless highspeed network, except in advertisements of these telecom companies. Above all, now both the government and the telecom providers are staring at each other for survival.

Snapshot of Telecom sector;

- Total subscriber base – 117.2 crore, as on December, 2019.

- Active Internet subscribers reached – 53 crore by 2018.

- India has the highest data usage per month per individual, at – 9.8 GB.

- Tele-density (number of telephone connections for every 100 individuals) was 90.11 percent in FY'19.

- Telecom sectors gross revenues stood at – US$33.97 billion in FY'19.

- There are over 62,443 uncovered villages in India.

- By October, 2019, the number of wallet transactions stood at – 3.59 billion. (IBEF, 2020)

- Telecom sector contributes 6.5% to India's GDP (Invest India, 2020).

The gross revenue for April – June 2019 was INR 61,535 crore (IBEF, 2020), and this roughly translates into INR 2.4 lakh crore annual revenues. And if we look at the debts owned by just two companies (Bharti Airtel and Vodafone-Idea), it amounts to Rs. 2.72 lakh crore (Sarkar, 2019) and if one looks at the debts of three companies ; Reliance Jio, Bharti Airtel & Vodafone-Idea, it is Rs. 3.90 lakh crore (Naidu, 2019). How on earth will these companies even think of surviving, leave alone rolling out 5G ?

Due to debt servicing, telecom companies must be finding it hard to invest in telecom infrastructure. Also, according to the Telecom Regulatory Authority of India (TRAI), "Gross Revenue (GR) declines from Rs. 2,55,655 crore in 2017 to Rs. 2,37,417 crore in 2018 with yearly decline rate of 7.13 percent. AGR also declines from Rs,1,60,814 crore in 2017 to Rs. 1,44,446 crore in 2018 with yearly decline rate of 10.18 percent" (PTI, 2019).

Wouldn't it be better if the telecom companies leased these airwaves on a 50:50 revenue sharing basis instead of an auction with an upfront payment ? For sure, had this revenue sharing been done, telecom companies would have invested in building world class infrastructure with good quality services, thereby increasing their gross revenues as well. Moreover, the government could have made lakhs of crore from the revenue sharing on a perpetual basis.

The way forward

Government must introspect the 'sudden death' of this enabler of the digital economy and where it went wrong. Also, the following may help bring the telecom sector back on track:

- 5G network is being designed for less than 1 millisecond latency and India must develop *'FG (Future Generation)'* technology, which must be a step ahead of 5G.

- We need to set up an independent body — the 'Futuristic Technology Mission *(FTM)'* — a joint initiative of DST, DRDO, ISRO, IITs, C-DAC, C-DOT, NITI Aayog and Start-up India, and give them a corpus of Rs. 5,000 crore to develop a FG solution in the next 600 days. I believe, we have what it takes to achieve the seemingly impossible by 2021.

- Today, the world is trying to sell the 5G technology to India, but if we develop our own technology in the next three years, countries would line up to use India's FG technology, like they use ISROs' satellite launch vehicle to put their satellites into orbit.

- Success of FG technology will also boost the original equipment manufacturer (OEM) market for FG — IOT devices in India, and catalyse Indian industries and add tremendous power to brand India. We have a once-in-a-century opportunity. Let us not fritter it away by becoming digital slaves of the First World.

- Let us not undermine our talent. Let us leverage this lifetime opportunity to put India atop the global map. It is safe to assume that this country can deliver it and if all the right assistance is provided, better than most others. Provide the money, repose trust and keep the bureaucracy out. Indians should not be labelled as a bunch of body shopping H1B visa seekers. (Gupta R.P., DNA, 2019)

Also, India must henceforth replace all telecom airwaves auctions with revenue sharing model of 50:50 basis and this must be on the gross revenue sharing. Private sector should make profits but not profiteer out of sovereign wealth. They must create value driven business models which deliver profits and increase the usage of telecom, and boost businesses and productivity. With revenue sharing, one important impact will be that, the Government will get a recurrent income every year to manage its finances. Auction is the simplest way to kill the goose which could lay golden eggs for decades to come and also, Indigenous 5G technology will be a big boost to home grown entrepreneurs (Start-Up India) for creating a robust IOT system around the 5G technology, which could add billions of dollars to the economy, given that we are looking at building smart cities.

Sustainable Automation

'Automation' will enhance quality and inequality, but 'Sustainable Automation' will balance quality and equality'

The world over, post COVID-19, there will be a shift to automation to boost profitability and avoid over dependence on manual labour, and this 'contagion' will spread to all levels, across sectors. With companies increasingly becoming investor driven, who are looking at ROI (Return On Investment) in these hyper competitive times, automation will percolate down soon. *India, as a nation, must adopt 'Responsible' and 'Sustainable Automation', which not only includes 'Proliferation of technology for Profits' but also for 'People'. 'People' have to be an integral part of the equation.* As I analyse the data and trends on automation and machine learning, it is clear that, *'Technology will drive quality and inequality'. So, 'Sustainable and Responsible Automation' should be like our SDG#18, as an intergenerational goal across sectors.*

This is not futuristic! Already automation has started in India. For example, the Tata Motors manufacturing plant for 'Harrier' vehicle has been able to achieve 90 percent automation (Gupta R.P., Your Vote is

Not Enough – A Citizen's Charter to Making a Difference, 2019).

For a country like India, which needs 10 lakh new jobs/month for people entering the job market, indiscriminate automation can lead to social unrest with economic instability. We have to develop a frame-work for 'Sustainable Automation' as an inter-generational goal, and ensure that it is adhered to. We need to ensure job for every hand.

Planning

Given the delicate situation we are in, and the failure of NITI Aayog to help India predict the slowdown, leave alone arrest the slowdown, it is time for relooking at NITI Aayog, and making it a forecasting, planning and consultancy body of the Government.

We need to give up the five year – 'election based' planning, and create an intergeneration plan for the next quarter of the century. We need a broader vision for India, which is further broken down into yearly plans to be reviewed every quarter, and the findings put in public domain, and tabled in the parliament. In 2018, NITI Aayog released a report on Artificial Intelligence and posted the fancy report with a lot of media coverage. We are not sure if this report was even used during the COVID-19 crisis! A 'National Think Tank' body's job is not to produce academic reports and author articles for media, but to give a direction to the ministries on how best to be prepared to handle such exigencies.

There must be sectoral experts who must be a part of such think tanks. If our planning is right, and implementation guided by sectoral experts, we can grow our GDP by additional fifty percent. This calls for acknowledging the problem at the highest level and taking appropriate action. Also, NITI Aayog should not be chaired by the Prime Minister. It should be an independent body with clear cut deliverables, defined by the Prime Minister/Government.

Immediate Steps – Post COVID

Given our experience with COVID-19, in any such national exigency, the first important step for the government is to access the situation realistically and make plans keeping the worst-case scenario in mind, and then plan for the financial relief package. Our economy has suffered a massive hit, and we should first dissect which segments have suffered the most, and what is the way to get them back on track. Industries are, by and large, organized and there are trade lobbies which will find their way into the system by tweaking the rules and relief in their favour. But the real impactful action would be, if we are able to regain the trust of people who don't have a voice – the small farmers, unorganized and migrant workers, shop-keepers, SHGs, and MSMEs. One – there is financial loss due to lockdown, and two – is the loss of human resources and their trust in the government to support them in the times of need. COVID-19 is no ordinary crisis. For many of us, it is a 'Never happened before' crisis, and it is also not the last crisis we are facing this year or that our worries end after this crisis is over. So, the government will have to put a system in place to prepare for any such future eventuality and simultaneously initiate a mega program to rebuild the economy, and rekindle the trust in the government.

Financial Loss

If we look at the key sectors which contribute to the GDP & Jobs, and are impacted by COVID-19, the scenario appears grim on the job and the GDP growth front:

	Sector	Contribution to GDP (%)	Employment (Millions)	Minimum Expected Decline (my assessment from the data)
1	Automobile	7.1	35	25%
2	Auto components	2.3	3	25%
3	Apparel & Textiles	2.3	45	30%
4	Consumer, retail and internet	10	8% of employment	20%
5	MSME	30–35	114	40%
6	Aviation	2.4	42.7	50%
7	Tourism	9.2		

Data source: (KPMG, 2020) & https://www.investindia.gov.in/

The biggest challenge COVID-19 has posed to the industry is the closure of about two months, and these months are important. March is the end of the financial year and April is the start of the financial year. Also that, most of the companies operate on a sub-ten percent profit margin, and this is going to reflect in their two financial years – the one that has gone by, and the one that has just started. For sure, some of the businesses will be under a severe cash crunch and will shut down.

Zero Quarter

Ideally, for the government, it would have been better to declare a 'Zero Quarter', and waive all taxes and compliances for the month of March, April and May 2020 (except the annual returns), and extend a line of credit to businesses for six months of their working capital, or interest free loans subject to certain pre-defined criteria. But both the government and the businesses will find it tough to get this implemented, as both have not trusted each other for long. Yet, there are ways in which this can be implemented and may provide a lifeline to MSMEs and small traders.

Human Resources

It is a known fact that ninety percent of the workers are in the unorganized sector, and they are a major contributor to the industry as manual labour, be it; construction, travel and tourism, security, farming, small establishments, etc. The movement of unorganized labour would be a massive loss, and this is where the impact will on the continuity of (especially) small businesses be more severe and can be debilitating to the economy. Even for the sake of assumption, if we consider that 30% of the workers have moved back to their places of residence, or will move back to their home state once this interstate lockdown is lifted, it would mean that the business establishments which employed them will find it hard to bring them back immediately. So effectively, migrant workers are not returning before August.

I recall the situation in Maharashtra more than a decade ago, when non-Maharashtrians were forced to go back to their home states. Builders had to delay their projects by six months to a year as they did not have the labourers. Post COVID-19, the situation is grimmer than what happened in Maharashtra. This time, the impact will be felt all over India. Due to lockdown, majority of labourers have been stuck in the middle, and not been able to reach home, and about 25 percent of these labourers may not return to the towns to work. This is certainly not a good sign and clearly indicates that the government will have to take some steps like setting up the Worker's Township (CENTER – mentioned ahead), and even provide free train travel for such workers to come and find work in towns, to address the issues related to the unorganised and migrant labourers displacement.

If we look at the table below titled, 'Reasons for migration of Rural-Urban Migrants, 2001–2011', work and study appear to be the key drivers for migration of males, and for females it is marriage. But while the females migrate for marriage, they may start working in the new place of settlement.

Reasons for migration of Rural-Urban Migrants, 2001, 2011 (all durations)

	Male					Female				
	Work*	Study	Family*	Others	Total	Work*	Study	Family*	Others	Total
Total in 2011	49.7%	4.1%	36.4%	9.9%	100%	5.1%	2.0%	86.5%	6.4%	100%
Total in 2001	55.2%	3.7%	27.8%	13.3%	100%	4.1%	1.2%	85.3%	9.3%	100%
Within district	42.2%	5.5%	35.2%	17.0%	100%	3.1%	1.6%	85.7%	9.6%	100%
Other districts within State	54.7%	4.4%	28.3%	12.7%	100%	4.7%	1.2%	84.6%	9.5%	100%
Inter-State	66.6%	1.6%	21.1%	10.7%	100%	5.0%	0.6%	85.8%	8.6%	100%

Source: Census of India 2001, 2011 (*work/employment and business and marriage, moved after birth and moved with household have been consolidated into work and family respectively) Each of the rows (separately for male and female) will add to 100, subject to rounding errors.

According to the census of India 2011, there were 454 million migrants within India (Ministry of Housing and Urban Poverty Alleviation, 2017, p. 5)

From the table titled, 'Share of Migrant Workers in Total Workers by Major Sectors' appended below, we find that almost all major sectors, be it; agriculture, or manufacturing, or services – employ migrants, and are going to take a severe hit.

Share of Migrant Workers in Total Workers by Major Sectors

Sector*	Rural		Urban	
	Male	Female	Male	Female
Primary	4%	75%	20%	65%
Manufacturing	13%	59%	38%	51%
Public Services	16%	69%	40%	56%
Construction	8%	73%	32%	67%
Traditional Services	10%	65%	29%	55%
Modern Services	16%	66%	40%	52%
Total	**6%**	**73%**	**33%**	**56%**

Source: NSS 2007-08 * Using the National Industrial Classification codes of 2004 (NIC) **Primary** includes agriculture, hunting, forestry, fishing, mining and quarrying (NIC 01-14), **Manufacturing** is NIC 15-37, **Public Services** are NIC 40-41, Transport via Railways (NIC 6010), National Postal activities (NIC 64110), and Public Administration (NIC 751, 752 and 753), **Construction** is NIC 45), **Traditional services** include wholesale and retail trade, hotels and restaurants, transport, storage and communications (NIC 50-52, 55, 60-64, except 6010 and 64110), and **Modern services** includes Financial Intermediation, Real estate, renting and business, education, health, social work, other community, social and personal services (NIC 65-74, 80, 85, 90-99, excluding 751, 752, 753).

(Ministry of Housing and Urban Poverty Alleviation, 2017, p. 7).

"According to the NSS 64th round, about 43% of Delhi's population are migrants, with over half coming from Uttar Pradesh and Bihar, two of India's less developed states. While all migrants to Delhi are from out of state, there is a difference between migrants who come from rural and urban areas. Typically, migrants from rural areas tend to be more employed in manufacturing and traditional services, i.e. trade, hotels, transportation, etc., while those from urban areas are employed in public services like health and education and also in modern services like real estate, financial intermediation, information technology, etc."

"Mumbai also has 43% of its population as migrants, with over half of out-of-state migrants also coming from Uttar Pradesh and Bihar and over a quarter of recent migrants from within state, a proportion which has fallen over the years. The jobs picture is different between these two groups. In addition to manufacturing and traditional services, migrants from rural Maharashtra are also likely to find employment in public and social services, more so than urban migrants from other states. They are less concentrated in modern business services. However, for rural migrants from out of state, the pattern is similar to Delhi, with more concentration in manufacturing and traditional services, and less in public services" (Ministry of Housing and Urban Poverty Alleviation, 2017, p. 11).

The Way Forward

It is for sure that the migrants are in a state of shock. They faced a dilemma of choosing between, 'Lives and Livelihood', and a large number of migrants chose 'Lives' and decided to move back to their hometowns, because they understood the fact that, with family, they can manage the basics of life in their village. This will lead to a new 'reality in rural India', when some of such families decide not to return back to the towns. The workers chose 'Lives' and now, it's the government's responsibility to make provisions for their 'Livelihood. So, it is a unique challenge for the central and state government as, on one side, rural public distribution system will be burdened, and on the other side, the sectors in urban areas which depend on these labourers will be on the verge of closure. Given the experience of this 'Great Lockdown', it will require not just an assurance, but a lot more. For this to happen, the governments at the state and the centre need to implement innovative ideas and mega schemes to rebuild India. In a sense, COVID-19 will act as a leveler and give us an opportunity to focus on an inward-looking model, and will be a catalyst for building a strong India.

Some of the transformative ideas needed to build the 'New India' are mentioned in the section ahead.

Innovative Ideas to Transform & Rebuild India

Distributed Growth Model

A New Economic Model

COVID-19 has shown how strong and vibrant economies can become fragile. Such a crisis has no precedent, and the leaders will be measured for their success in saving jobs, and avoiding business closures, while at the same time, holding the economy together and preventing it from collapsing. This is the toughest time to be at the helm of affairs, and an astute leader would utilize this 'once in a lifetime opportunity' to usher in major reforms, and build a new economic model. The task at hand is not easy, but a leader who uses an innovative approach to sail the nation out of this COVID-19 crisis, will prove his mettle to the world.

COVID-19 has created such a scenario that everyone, except for the government employees, are uncertain about the future of jobs and income. A two months lockdown can have devastating impact on lower-middle income, and middle-income families. Even some upper-middle income and rich families, who have built business on debt, can face severe losses and go out of business. Some of the sectors that will feel the impact:

- Unsold inventory of two and four wheelers will be tough to liquidate, and with stocks piling up, and with new emission norms (BS VI) kicking in, the spiraling affect will be too much for automotive companies to handle.

- The telecom sector is passing through an existential crisis due to the mounting debt, and under the given circumstances, we must forget 5G for a while.

- Divestment of Air India would be a tough task as the entire travel and tourism sector will remain subdued for many more quarters, and the profitability of this sector will remain weak, right until 2022.

- Construction segment will remain under duress and if they have taken loans from the banks, a high possibility is that these loans could turn into NPAs.

- Small businesses dependent on the migrant manpower are worst hit. Manpower is gone for most of them, while rentals and other routine expenses keep piling up.

- We will have to be prepared for the NRIs/workers abroad, who will be returning back to India, and look for jobs or starting a business.

- Sales pipeline for large corporates would be dry for now.

- Non-essential categories will feel the maximum pain, and the even the essential categories will see about 20 percent decline.

- Luxury goods market though will feel the impact, but not much, as the buyers are basically HNIs (High Net worth Individuals), and they are not impacted to the extent to which the middle class is impacted. Few HNIs may have suffered losses, but they have stashed enough cash to last them through the *'COVIDepression'* (long phase of recession post COVID-19).

Only silver lining for India is its farming population. Despite all the setbacks, agriculture so far has not suffered much, and this means our crop yield and farming output is going to keep us sailing, though rural spending will come down, which now a days is a major focus area for FMCG and even companies in other sectors. This is the time for India to take a conscious call on – What fundamentals it wishes to build the Future Economy on? I would strongly recommend the *'Distributed Growth Model – The MAST Model'.*

The *Distributed Growth Model* is based on the fundamental premise that focussing on large number of small entities makes a more equitable and robust economic society than focusing on a small number of large entities. I started writing about it in 2015 (Gupta R.P., Can Make In India Learn From Make It In Germany, 2015), and I coined the term *'Distributed Growth Model'* in 2017 in my article 'Distributed Growth

Model Is the Need of The Hour. Growth Alone Will Not Suffice' (Gupta R.P., Opinion, 2018). The article was published in January, 2018, and since then, I have written about it in various articles and also mentioned about it in my earlier book, 'Your Vote is Not Enough'.

MAST Model

The *Distributed Growth Model* is built on the four pillars of the production and consumption economy, *viz.*

1. **MSME** – Micro, Small and Medium Enterprises

2. **Agriculture** and Allied sectors

3. **Self** Help Groups – SHGs

4. **Traders** – Co-operatives & Solo-entrepreneurs

We have to focus on each of these four categories to build and sustain the economy. India has a great opportunity post-COVID-19 to redesign its economic landscape, and to me, this is the best time in our country's history to make a switch. Anything other than focusing on the above – mentioned four-pillars would be a recipe for long-term disaster, which will increase the divide between the 'haves and have nots'. India, with about 135 crore population, cannot afford to mess up in choosing its economic model.

This is the model which will make the wealth generation broad-based, and will also boost and equalize consumption on one hand, and on the other hand, de-risk the economy by broad basing and decentralizing it. This needs a careful action plan, including key partnerships amongst the Ministries of: Finance, Agriculture, Rural Development, MSME, Tourism, and Women & Child Development. It is not just about these ministries coming together, but also about them partnering to build an ecosystem with a new economic model which hitherto has not been tried elsewhere, i.e. the MAST Model.

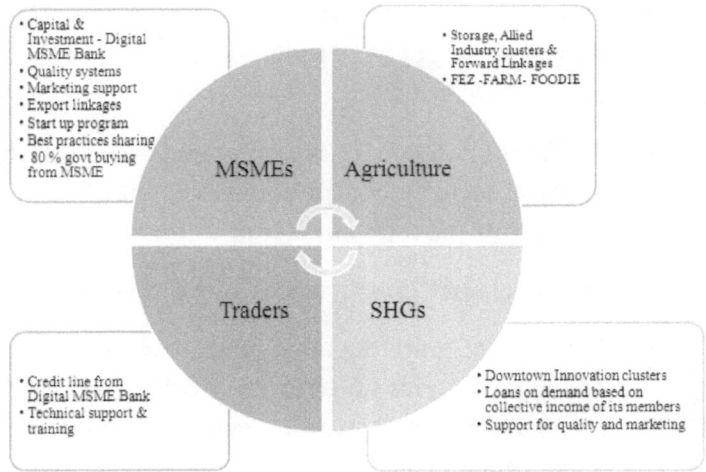

- Capital & Investment - Digital MSME Bank
- Quality systems
- Marketing support
- Export linkages
- Start up program
- Best practices sharing
- 80 % govt buying from MSME

MSMEs   **Agriculture**

- Storage, Allied Industry clusters & Forward Linkages
- FEZ -FARM- FOODIE

Traders   **SHGs**

- Credit line from Digital MSME Bank
- Technical support & training

- Downtown Innovation clusters
- Loans on demand based on collective income of its members
- Support for quality and marketing

MSME

India has about 7.5 crore MSMEs, providing employment to 11.4 crore people and contributing to between 30–35 per cent of the GDP (KPMG, 2020, p. 47).

We need to learn lessons from Germany, a strong and a resilient economy, which remained relatively untouched by the recession of 2008. The key to this country's success is Mittelstand – a policy approach, in which SMEs receive state patronage and support, and they, in turn, make the biggest contribution to high employment and productivity. Here are some interesting statistics (Ref: Business – Growth – Prosperity by Federal Ministry of Economics and Technology, Germany);

- More than 99 per cent of all German firms (3.7 million) belong to the SME category.

- SMEs contribute almost 52 per cent of the total economic output of Germany, totaling a turnover of 2 trillion euros.

- SMEs employs 60 per cent of workforce, subject to social security contributions, and take in 83.2 per cent of the total number of trainees hired.

- 95 per cent of Germany's SMEs are family-owned.

- German SMEs are the most innovative in Europe and supply goods all over the world. There are some 1,300 world market leaders among the SMEs which make up the Mittelstand.

- These market leaders are in a variety of sectors, ranging across electrical, engineering and industrial products.

- The Mittelstand SMEs are a major contributor to a lower percentage of unemployed youth in Germany, as compared to many other European nations.

- The website www.make-it-in-germany.com is dedicated to the Mittelstand initiative.

How do we implement a successful, working replica of the Mittelstand model in India? To start with, we must have a clear plan to link MSME with agriculture. We need to invest heavily in innovation and quality upgradation of these MSMEs. We have to ensure that the products from these establishments meet the highest standards of quality. These enterprises be based predominantly in small towns across the country, and in Farmland Parks, and they need to be supported – not just with finances, but with strategy, marketing and export linkages, to ensure that not only their products and services are at par with the best in the world, but also available all throughout the globe. Most importantly, the government should mandate that 60 percent of all the government orders should go to MSMEs, else, MNCs will beat the MSMEs hands down. This is one reason why the full potential of MSMEs has not been realised in India. Without a clear roadmap, training and stringent quality control, the replication of the Mittelstand model will not take off. Entrepreneurs will take the loans made available to them, start their businesses, and in the absence of market knowledge and guidelines, fail – seek fresh loans, fail again – and get into a vicious cycle of debt. Or their loans will become non-performing assets (NPA) for the lenders, creating a bubble which could be much bigger than even farm loans. MSMEs must be supported under DEFA and the DREAM project (mentioned in detail further ahead), the vision for MSME being that – 60 percent of all jobs be provided by MSME sector, and they should be the strongest pillar, after agriculture, in terms of employment and contribution to GDP.

Agriculture

'We owe our cultivators a debt, payment for which is long overdue'.

Farmers/farming, and rural development are two sides of the same coin. Though we had a minor decline in the previous year in agricultural exports, but 58% population is still dependent on agriculture. About US$ 265.51 billion or Rs. 18.55 lakh crore worth of Gross Value Added came from Agriculture, Forestry and Fishing, supporting 13% of the total exports, and growing at CAGR of 16.45%. India currently exports to about 100 countries and 6 percent of the total Industrial investment is in agriculture (IBEF, 2020).

India has phenomenal natural assets for agriculture – India has the 10th largest arable land resource in the world, with 20 Agri-climatic regions. All major 15 climates in the world exist in India, along with 46 of the 60 global soil types (IBEF, 2020, p. 3), and the total length of 445 rivers flowing through the country is two lakh kilometres (Sirohi, 2018).

Agriculture is an issue of national security and our biggest insurance against economic insecurity, but it is gradually declining in terms of farmer's interest. If we focussed on agriculture as one of the key fundamentals of Indian economy, we will be insulated from global catastrophes. Even after the adverse impact of COVID-19, India as a nation, will be saved from recession, only due to its agrarian economy. But certainly, if we have to emerge stronger as an economy, we will need to take steps to strengthen and support agriculture, along with the rural economy, to ensure that agriculture is not only profitable, but also attractive. The population engaged in agriculture has continuously declined since 1951 (FAO, 2020). According to the Indian Economy Survey, agriculture's contribution to national income has gradually declined from 18.2 per cent in 2014–15 to 16.5 in 2019–20 (Ministry of Finance, Government of India, 2020).

While MSP (Minimum Support Price) for Agriculture Produce is the key strategy adopted by the Government to enhance the profitability of agriculture, but this will not be enough, as we have focussed only on profitability of agriculture in isolation, and not on the overall quality of life. So, we have to address both – the profitability of agriculture and the quality of life of the people in agriculture. Let us not forget that, farmers played an important role in the freedom struggle (BBC, 2017), and today, they are struggling for their existence! *We owe our cultivators a debt, payment for which is long overdue.* We need to make agriculture an attractive profession, along with ensuring a quality of life which is at par with the best, and the success of which will be proven when we are successful in reversing the trend of people moving away from agriculture – to people moving towards agriculture – and reversing the migration of people from rural areas to urban, and all this is doable!

Considering that automation is happening at a crazy pace in other sectors, it will be next to impossible to move the huge number of people engaged in agriculture into other jobs. And so, we should focus on profitability of agriculture and quality of life in the countryside, as it supports a huge segment of our population and can support much higher numbers, leading to a more equitable society, besides a vibrant economy.

India is the largest producer of spices, pulses, milk, tea, cashew and jute, and the second largest producer of wheat, rice, fruits and vegetables, sugarcane, and cotton and oilseeds. India has the largest livestock population of around 535.78 million, which is about 31% of the world population.

With 157 million hectares of arable agriculture land, and with improvement in storage facilities, now we have 1303 cold storage with 45 lakh tonne capacity (IBEF, 2020, p. 5). Marine products, buffalo meat, and rice are the largest agricultural export items in terms of value. Other major items are spices, cotton, oil products and sugar (IBEF, 2020, p. 11).

As of 2019, 18 out of the 40 approved food parks are operational in the country (IBEF, 2020, p. 32).

If we look at the Indian food industry and food processing industry, it seems to be pretty strong as is evident from the chart below:

Indian Food Industry in 2018 (US$ Billion		Infrastructure for Food Processing Industry (as of 2019)	
Food Industry Output	258	Cold Storage	133
Food Exports	39.4	Cold Storage capacity (Lakh Metric Tonne)	45.62
Food Imports	24.5	Mega Food Parks Sanctioned	39
Retail	380	Agri Export Zones	60
Food Service	48.3		

(IBEF, 2020, p. 13)

Areas of Concern and in need of Action

1. Plight of Farmers

The socio-economic census of 2011 revealed that; out of 24.39 crore families, 17.9 crore stay in rural areas, 36% of farmers according to NSSO are landless, the average monthly income of farmers in 2012–13 was Rs. 6426.00, and about 52–56% agriculture households are debt ridden, and farmers get only 20–30% of the retail prices (Sirohi, 2018). May be, we need to come to a situation where the government gives land to every landless farmer and ensures that a minimum 35% of the total GDP growth comes from agriculture and allied industries.

The report on agricultural indebtedness by NABARD further paints a grim picture of this sector (Nair, 2018).

- One in two households save, and the average savings is Rs. 9104.00.

- One in ten households invest, and the average investment is Rs. 62,734.00.

- One in two households have Indebtedness, and the average outstanding debt is Rs. 91407.00.

- One in four households have an insurance coverage.

- One in five households have pension cover.

Poultry contributes about 11.9% to the monthly farmers income, and 86% of the farmers are small and marginal (Sirohi, 2018).

A comparison across two time periods, 2004–05 and 2011–12, indicates that while there was an increase in the size of the total workforce in the country, the size of the agricultural workforce reduced by 30.57 million people. The share of agricultural workforce in total workforce declined from 56.7% to 48.8% in the same period.

2. Farm Holding

As much as 67 percent of India's farmland is held by the marginal farmers with holdings below one hectare, against less than 1 percent in large holdings of 10 hectares and above. The average size of the holding has been estimated as 1.15 hectare. The average size of these holdings has shown a steady declining trend over various Agriculture Censuses since 1970–71.

3. Irrigation

Another cause for concern is that, in 2010–11, the proportion of net irrigated area to net area sown was 45.70 percent, which shows that for half the country's farmland, irrigation is yet to reach farmers, who rely entirely on rains for their crops and so, we need to invest in rain water conservation and irrigation, as half of the arable land does not have irrigation facilities.

The area under irrigated land has a productivity (grains) of 4.00 ton/hectare, whereas the rain fed agricultural areas have a productivity of 1.2 ton/hectare (Sirohi, 2018).

4. Productivity

Agricultural productivity in India, considering that we have been traditionally an agrarian economy, is low when compared to other countries, as is evident from data below and this needs an immediate attention.

- In India, the average yield of grains per hectare is 3.62 ton, whereas in China it is 6.74 ton, Vietnam it is 5.75 ton.

- The average yield of wheat is 3.03 ton per hectare in India, whereas in France, it is 7.36 ton per hectare, and in China, it is 5.04 ton per hectare

- In India, the yield of corn is 2.75 ton per hectare, whereas in the USA, it is 10.73 ton/hectare and in Argentina, it is 6.6 ton/hectare

- For pulses, the yield per hectare in India is 6.54 quintal per hectare, whereas in Canada, it is 20.30 quintal per hectare, and in China, it is 15.5 quintal per hectare (Sirohi, 2018)

Decline of agriculture in Punjab is a glaring example and a wakeup call for India. Punjab, which was once known for green revolution with its majority of the population dependent on agriculture, is witnessing a decline in agriculture's contribution to GDP. From a high of 32.67% in 2004–05, agriculture's contribution to GDP has fallen to 21.83% (advance estimates) (Roy, 2013). Policy makers have to ensure that what happened in Punjab does not get repeated elsewhere in India and a top down approach is not the right one for India.

Few important points;

- A large portion of the population is dependent on agriculture.

- Majority of the farmland holdings is small, i.e. below 1 hectare and the average farm size is 1.5 hectare.

- Less than half of the farm lands have access to irrigation and depend on rains.

- Also, the farmlands/farmers are not connected to food-processing and other value-added opportunities for their farmland/produce.

- Various news reports and anecdotal evidences highlight the impact of labour shortage on some of these major crops, across various states.

- According to KPMG/NSSO analysis, there has been a shift of the agriculture workforce to non-agriculture sectors in the following secondary and tertiary sectors. The Primary sector comprising of: Agriculture, fisheries, forestry.

  Secondary: Mining, Manufacturing, Construction, Electricity – gas – steam, and air conditioning supply, Water supply – sewerage – waste management and remediation activities.

  Tertiary: Wholesale and retail trade, Repair of motor vehicles and motorcycles, Transportation and storage, Financial and insurance activities, etc.

- Only 0.65% students enroll in agriculture, and agriculture education and research need a quantum leap (Sirohi, 2018).

In the 11th Century, India's agricultural productivity was four tonnes per hectares and 25% of the population was engaged in trade (Sirohi, 2018). If corporates enter farming, then the income of farmers will not go up, unless they enter into food processing and logistics. What British did to agriculture, we are just continuing the same policies. We need to be cautious of what happened in America. In the 20th century, 30 million (3 crore) people were engaged in agriculture and in 21st century, due to mechanization, 89% of the agricultural production is done by a mere 3 lakh people, and if we follow the same system, farmers and rural India will not only become poorer, but it will create a burden (infrastructural, economic and social) on urban India, which urban India cannot handle.

Agriculture subsidy has increased to Rs. 73000 crores in the 2015/16 budget and in addition, the subsidy on agriculture loans is also about Rs. 15000 crores. (Sirohi, 2018). In addition, there is an increasing trend of waiving farm loans as an 'Electoral Proposition', as witnessed during the state elections, but it does not provide a solution to security, productivity, profitability and attractiveness of the farming profession. Moreover, ignoring these issues will have a direct impact on the country's rural development and the 'consumption index' or 'buying power' of India. Even increasing the MSP (Minimum Support Price) does not help in the short or the medium term and might backfire, as the farmers will have to produce the crops first, and then the government will have to ensure adequate storage, transport and prompt payment for the purchases made on MSP. So, while these announcements appear to catch the eye, but they are at best, an ad hoc arrangement, and not a permanent solution to problems resulting from the long-standing systemic shortfalls faced by the farming community. 'Political' loan waivers will lead to serious financial crisis and it has already set a wrong precedent. Tomorrow, people may ask for loan waivers under the Mudra scheme and this can trigger a massive crisis. We need a clear national loan deferment policy, and under which conditions and how much loan or its interest can be deferred, and how does the government make up for the loss ? Let us not close our eye to the fact that, for a large country with 1.35 billion people, food security is the key to economic & social security, and hence, the issue of farmers and farming have to be addressed, keeping in mind the wider issues, and the impending deeper crisis in agriculture and rural India. So, just a one-time farm loan waiver will not solve the farmland crises. Farmers and planners need to be in constant dialogue at the field level, and corrective steps cannot be just limited to a farm loan waiver during the election season, but the farmers need comprehensive plan to support the rural ecosystem.

Despite repeated attempts, the reason why the state of agriculture and status of farmers has not improved is because, we have overly become farming centric and issues around it, while upliftment of agriculture is a complex issue and is linked intricately to forward linkages and rural development, besides the recent developments in technology and allied industries related to agriculture. Increasing MSP will not solve the problem of agriculture in the long run and it is just a temporary pain killer. We have to look at a holistic solution and I have attempted to find a solution to our farmer's problem.

Comprehensive Solution for Agriculture:

Making agriculture an attractive vocation for the youth is the goal we should aspire and work for, and this calls for a new approach to look at for nurturing agriculture.

The vision: "An educated youth wearing jeans and t-shirt, listening music on tractor & happily tilling the land, a middle-aged farmer running a farm-guest house for tourists with all modern amenities & his wife and daughter running an enterprise selling handicrafts and local organic products nationally and internationally through the National eMarket". That's the vision for rural India; Agriculture – the future of highly profitable venture with quality of life!

The goal should be to make farming such an attractive profession/proposition for the youth of this country, that people start moving to agriculture. For rural development, the goal should be to attain a level of quality of life in rural India (countryside), so that reverse migration becomes a reality within a decade.

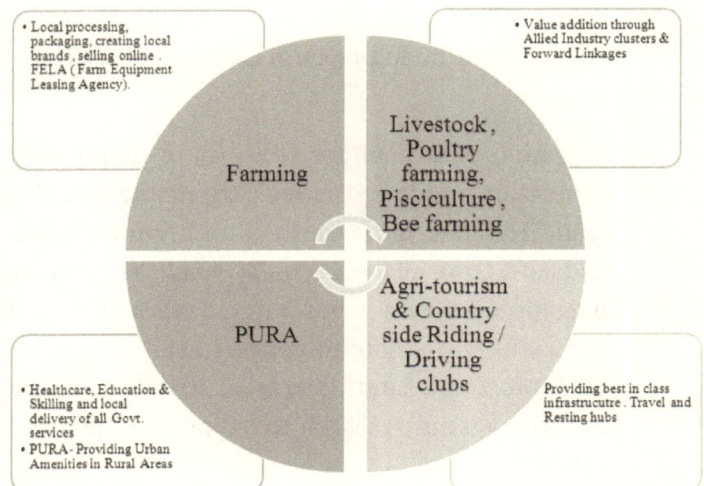

- Local processing, packaging, creating local brands , selling online . FELA (Farm Equipment Leasing Agency).

- Value addition through Allied Industry clusters & Forward Linkages

Farming

Livestock, Poultry farming, Pisciculture, Bee farming

PURA

Agri-tourism & Country side Riding / Driving clubs

- Healthcare, Education & Skilling and local delivery of all Govt. services
- PURA- Providing Urban Amenities in Rural Areas

Providing best in class infrastrucutre . Travel and Resting hubs

Suggestions

- Complete switch to Organic farming: India should become a 100 percent 'chemical free, non-GM (Genetically modified crops)', i.e., Organic agriculture country. This is the way forward for India to become the most valuable agricultural nation. The world over, people are moving towards organic produce, and India must avoid getting influenced by corporate lobbies, and switch to be an organic and non-GM crop nation, and focus on increasing agriculture productivity.

- Strategies have to be crop specific and region specific.

- Shortage and migration of labour force has to be addressed by including farm labour in MNAREGA scheme.

- Irrigation of agriculture land has to be pursued in mission mode by segregating arable and dry land; irrigated, non-irrigated, and rainfed areas, and an action plan has to be made to provide irrigation facilities to non-rainfed areas. Research is making it possible to convert even the desert land into arable land (Peerzada, 2018), and India has to invest in research to support agricultural productivity.

- Move from chemical fertilizers to herbicides.

- Crop insurance scheme must be implemented by the government at subsidized rates, or free.

- Farmers should get an advance line of credit before the sowing season, and then, they should get a subsistence allowance till the period of harvesting of the crops.

FELA - Farm Equipment Lending Agency

Farmers should be supported for high end implements, and tractors and other machines needed for agriculture. In fact, every District Farmers Co-operative or, *FELA (Farm Equipment Lending Agency)* should buy these implements, and maintain and lease them to farmers to reduce their cost of inputs, or farmers could come together and buy equipment and share. We need a national level institutional mechanism that can forecast and deploy the same as per need. This will also provide a boost to the manufacturing industry associated with agriculture.

KISAN - Krishak Information, Solution and Assistance Network

Ministry of Agriculture should develop a mobile app-based platform *(KISAN app)*. This app could take pictures of the area under cultivation (with type of crop sown), geotagging location, irrigation network, power network, and also connecting it to the local *'FELA' (Farm Equipment Lending Agency)*, where farmers can book, share, and lend farm equipment amongst the network. Also, this app could connect farmers to the nearest Farmer's Market or Weekend Market, should they want to directly sell to the consumers, or to the *NeM (National eMarket)*, if they wish to package it, and sell it online. Further, this app could use Artificial Intelligence tools, and guide the farmers, if their yield can be value added by connecting to the nearest food processing hub, and making a finished product, and how much more they could earn from their produce. Like; a millet farmer could package it into small packs and sell it; a sugarcane farmer can process it into organic jaggery powder or make fortified snacks at the nearest *MSME Innovation cluster (Farmland Park)* and create a brand for an organic produce to sell it online. This tool should also be able to help inform the farmer about the potential produce in the season and how much of the produce he could store in the nearest cold storage, based on the online booking available on 'KISAN'.

KISAN should be able to assist the farmer, based on his soil type, holding size and sowing seasons, the herbs farmers can sow during crop rotation, and how much income the farmer can add due to this, and also, link the farmer to the buyer of these herbs. Raw material for herbs is always in short supply. With this step of farmers taking to rotation farming of medicinal plants, India could become the world's biggest exporter of Ayurveda and natural products. For this, we need to have a mission mode project for medicinal plants and it is a big opportunity for India. This can add to the income of the farmers and help the Ayurveda manufacturers by forward linkages.

Based on the farmers or farm workers holding size, AI backed application can find additional attractive sources of income from poultry farming, or bee farming, or pisciculture, etc., and connect the farmer to the available government schemes for each of these opportunities. New skills and technologies can be made available to the farmers to improve productivity and their income. Those farmers who have the resources, can invest into setting a 'Farm Cottage' for Agri-tourism, and those who have land, but not resources, can actually work with the Ministry of Tourism. The KISAN app can be the platform to share authentic data while seeking assistance to develop 'Agri-Tourism' based on the AI tools assessment of the climate, access, and other criteria based on an algorithm. I don't think we need to worry about doubling farmer's income, if we are able to effectively implement the above. Certainly, MSP is not the solution for the farmer's problems. We need to implement 'KISAN' & 'FELA' and many more such propositions to make a difference.

FARM (Farmers and Agricultural Retail Marts)

Farmers co-operatives, who wish to set up Organic Super-markets – FARM, should be given allocated land in towns, or leased on an annual rent at lower than market rates. Government can also make up for the investment through the taxes and rentals it collects.

- Research should be intensified on increasing productivity and sustainability in agriculture, and the same should be shared through the 'KISAN' app. Also, based on the requirements of the farmers for newer techniques for increasing production and for innovations, the nearest agriculture universities should work with these farmers, and publish their work, with the farmer being the first author, and there should be a financial reward for this, besides recognition. As mentioned in my book, 'Your Degree is Not Enough – Education for GenNext', we must grant degrees equivalent to the knowledge of the farmer, based on their level of expertise (Gupta R.P., Your Degree is Not Enough – Education for GenNext, 2020, p. 152).

- Farmers should be trained and equipped with the necessary tools to manage the entire chain from farm to fork, and this is the one important step that will retain people in agriculture and make it worthwhile for them. This also calls for government investing in a major way in cold storage, processing, road and rail connectivity to the nearest towns, and providing an online marketing platform. Given that 7–13 percent (numbers vary from source to source) of exports is from agriculture, we need to enhance agricultural exports from the current 13 percent to 25 percent, to give a boost to rural India through agriculture.

- Crops like millets, which are vital for nutrition, should be given focus, and government should create an institutional set up for export of such crops, and promote them for domestic and international consumption through advertisements, to create a global market for such crops from India. It is time to do a 'branding' exercise for the crops from India, like 'Basmati' rice, and make each crop a multi-billion-dollar industry for farmers.

INKOM - International Kisan Operated Marts

The government should set up the 'Indian Farmers Holding Corporation' in major countries which will sell India's agricultural produce through INKOM – *International Kisan Operated Marts*. INKOMs would be like an international Indian Mandi for selling the produce in foreign markets operating round the year. This will not only enhance our export, but also give us a permanent footing in international markets for our agricultural produce.

- Organic farming should be given a major institutional support. We need an *Organic Farming Corporation of India* to give an institutional push to organic crops. We must resist the lobbying by the fertilizer, chemical industry, and the producers of genetically modified products. It is tough, but in the best and long-term interest of farmers.

- GM crops should be banned in India for farming and for sale, and there should be a special labelling (Black dot with GM written) on products that have genetically modified ingredients in it.

FEZ - Farmland Economic Zones & Farmland Parks

FEZ should be set up every 100 kilometers and within every district. The whole idea of FEZ (Farmland Park) is to have MSME enterprises, cold storage, food processing and packaging units in these 'Farmland Economic Zones'. Ideally, these should be located mid-way between the district and the agriculture farms.

They should include every opportunity for value addition to farmer's produce and must be promoted as a destination for travelers. FEZ (Farmland Park) should be the single point for processing, packaging and export, and also have 'FARM outlets' in the front, and an entertainment zone, including small theatre or Cinema theatres. The whole point of having them mid-way between districts and farms is that, people from the nearest town may drive down on weekends to pick up the produce directly, and the FEZ (Farmland Park) should become new economic hubs.

KARMA - (Krishi Aadharit Rozgar Mobile App)

This mobile based app should be specifically for Farm Labour and people seeking employment in agriculture and allied industries. This app must be initiated by Ministry of Agriculture and Rural Development.

RASTA (Riders Assistance Services and Transit Area)

By setting up the retail sale outlets at FEZ, we will encourage families to go on long drives and visit these FEZs. India being a country of youth, the riders club & driving clubs will grow over time, and become a major user base for RASTA, leading to enrichment of the local farm community. RASTA will act as the local rider's stop, and serve as 'assistance, rest area, and as a 'destination' point. This can be set up every 50 kilometers with cafés, restaurants, resting area, besides other service providers in such resting zones. Needless to mention, that the local farmland owners and workers association must operate these destination points, and all shops must be run by local communities.

Food-Fest

India is a land of phenomenal diversity in terms of crops, foods, spices etc. It is time to host an annual 'International Food Fest' round the year, on a rotation basis, but it should be running in every zone – North, East, West, South and Central. This festival should run like a *'Food Haat Festival'* with an option of street food stalls, and also restaurant dining experience with foods from all over India, the world's most exquisite cuisines being served, and packaged food also being sold. This can become a major tourist attraction, besides boosting the diversity and local economies and brands. The idea behind inviting international vendors is that, it can attract tourists to come and try global cuisine at this festival. Given that this festival is being hosted in India, we could allow fifty-sixty percent space for Indian cuisine, and the rest be shared for the global cuisine.

FOODIE (Farmland Operated Outlets of Domestic & International Eateries)

I have travelled to nearly thirty-five countries or perhaps more, and I have seen the craze for Indian food. May be, it is time for the Ministry of Agriculture, Ministry of Tourism and Ministry of External Affairs, to start putting the India Food Festival on the world map by hosting it in major tourist hot spots, round the year through FOODIE outlets in major international towns and at international airports. This initiative could be led by the Ministry of Tourism.

e-Government Service Centres (eGSCs)

With digitization being the sole medium of work during COVID-19, we must continue using these digital tools for conducting the office work post COVID-19 for eGovernance. It is time that we ensure that people from the Farmlands do not need to travel to towns at all for any work related to Government offices. All should be available online and through the e-Government Service Centres (eGSCs) established at the Farmland Parks. Also, district administration officials must spend 20 percent of their time visiting the e-GSCs and Farmlands to solve people's problem in their area.

- It is time to consider merging Ministry of Food Processing with Ministry of Agriculture.

- It is time we ban FDI in agriculture related activities like, Floriculture, Horticulture, Apiculture and Cultivation of Vegetables & Mushrooms; Development and production of Seeds and planting material; Animal Husbandry (including breeding of dogs), Pisciculture, Aquaculture, under controlled conditions; and Services related to agri and allied sectors, including Tea sector.

- At present, only farmers can buy agricultural land. Not immediately, but over the next three to five years, government should allow Indians (individuals), who wish to take to farming, to buy agricultural land.

'Happy Farmer – Prosperous India'

Rural India – Villages (Farmlands) as Economic Units

'Focus should be to make villages Self-sustainable & Self-sufficient Economic Units'.

With about $2/3^{rd}$ of India living in villages and dependent on agriculture, we should start calling rural area as 'Farmlands', so that, at least some sense of guilt will be followed by the desired action. It is a shame that, despite the Panchayati Raj and other schemes of the centre and states, the basic infrastructure for majority of the Indians (Indians living in villages) does not exist! The overarching theme of the government does not result in development, and has failed to bridge the divide between the so called 'Bharat' and 'India'. The aim should be to provide uniform access to all Indians to the same basic infrastructure. This not only needs immediate attention to correct our failure of seven decades, but also that, unlocking the hidden value of our 'farmlands' holds the secret to make India a developed country.

Since, 'Farmlands' have escaped industrialization, they still have clean environment – uncluttered and open space, and we should aim to build an infrastructure of connectivity, health, and education in rural India, and also ensure that, all government services offered in towns are available through the e-Government Service Centres (eGSCs). We must aim that the reverse migration starts by 2025. Else, we would have failed majority of the population in our being over-zealousness to provide the best of infrastructure in urban areas.

We should invest more in rural and semi-urban areas to make them attractive destination for reverse migration. I still recall that we had this oft-repeated political slogan in Maharashtra, 'We will make Mumbai like Shanghai'. But this should not have been the aim at all. We should have tried to make smaller towns 'Mini Mumbai' or 'Chandigarh'. Rather than trying to ape the mega-metros, it might be a better idea to identify focus towns/countryside (farmlands) in each state, and invest in their development. Big towns should henceforth get funds only for maintenance, or become self-sufficient in generating their own resources over the next five years.

Villages need to have a sustainable model for economy, infrastructure and environment, and it should not just be sustainable and self-sufficient, but also attractive for the urban population to start moving towards countryside (farmland) for settling down. Nearest town should not be more than a 40 minute drive from any village (excluding hilly terrains). We should be able to come out with a model that eliminates the difference between rural and urban areas based on infrastructure (roads, electricity, internet and cellular services, education, health and government services) this is where PURA is needed (Providing Urban Amenities in Rural Areas). We need "Smart and self-sufficient villages clusters", as all villages are not having adequate population for making them self-sustainable. Village level self-sufficiency means that value addition – linked to agriculture produce, should happen in villages, and not in urban areas, based on the solution provided above. If we focus on food processing in bigger towns only, then the urban-rural divide will grow further, and not lessen. We need a plan for building world class SMEs in food/agriculture produce processing, handicrafts etc., within FEZs, and link them to the nation through online sales platform for direct supplies to retailers or consumers. Hence, we need enough packaging units in rural India, with logistic facilities, including road connectivity, so that farmers are able make the best use of modern development to have higher profits. Also, besides economic avenues for rural India, we need to make life more vibrant, and for that to happen, we need to ensure proper avenues for sports, culture and arts, entertainment, health and eGSCs, within a self-contained FEZ, backed by a solar farm. The success of all these steps will result in more and more people turning to agriculture and moving to the countryside (farmlands) because of the quality of life and earning capacity.

Various ministries like Agriculture, Rural Development, Transport, Tourism, Women & Child Development, Renewable Energy, and MSME, must work hand-in-hand to uplift the Indian economy in an equitable manner. There has to be an overarching vision of these ministries for rural integration for the upliftment of the farmlands. Else, working in silos wouldn't deliver, despite investments!

We should understand the basic fact that, the current model of generating income in urban areas through large corporates and then distributing the benefits (taxes collected), will not work. In fact, those whom we consider as beneficiaries (Farmers & Farmlands), have to become wealth creators.

Thanks to the proliferation of media channels and cheap data, now rural India also sees what the mega metros watch, and hence, there is fire in their belly. Rural India today is more aspirational. If we provide them the right support system, they will deliver big in every sphere of economic opportunity. We just need to support them adequately.

Farmland Park (FEZ) should now become the economic hubs for creating jobs and driving the next level of growth – in double digits, which is sustainable enough for the next quarter of the century to transform India into a developed nation by 2045. Post that, we need not worry about growth curve anymore as we should become self-sufficient and sustainable.

SHGs (Self Help Groups)

Government aims to bring one woman from each rural household in the ambit of the scheme for SHGs, and the target is to include nine crore women, aiming at their socio-economic development. As on 31st May 2019, 5.96 crore women have been mobilised into 54.07 lakh women Self Help Groups (SHGs) under the Deen Dayal Antyodaya Yojana (PIB, Government of India, 2019)

The Government of India is promoting Self Help Groups (SHGs) for realization of socio-economic development through its programs. Women can get loans up to Rs. 2.5 Lakh under the government scheme. It is time to take the programs to the next level, and link up the SHGs on VKAP (*Vishwakarma program – mentioned ahead)*, give them loan from the Digital MSME bank, link them to the downtown clusters in *FEZ*, and also, give them the opportunity to run community kitchens and community stores in the *CENTER (Community Enterprise Township & Enclave for Residents – mentioned ahead)*. SHGs have phenomenal potential and we must now move from being an NGO model for SHGs, to a commercial model – where they must be given an opportunity to help ideate and spin off commercial businesses. Lijjat Papad Udhyog is a model to look at and replicate. We must support SHGs through the *REWARD program (Resident Entrepreneur With Attractive and Replicable Demo – mentioned ahead)* and *DREAM (District Retail & Employment Analysis And Marketing – mentioned ahead)* projects at *DEFA (District Employment and Entrepreneurship Facilitation Agency – mentioned ahead)*.

Best practices based on success stories of SHGs should be shared. A SHG YouTube channel in multiple languages – with subtitles in local languages, would be a good way to promote the work, and encourage more women to form SHGs. This is not about poor or poverty, but also empowerment, and SHGs can play a pivotal role in nurturing local economy.

Small Traders and Retail Stores

With about 1.4 crore (numbers vary as per various estimates) retailers across the length and breadth of India, the country's consumer and employment markets are, in a way, dependent on this trade channel. The worst decision of successive governments has been to open the retail and wholesale market to Foreign Direct Investment (FDI). Large-scale retailers are unwelcomed even in the largest, most developed economies, and most locals have problems with them for their role in squeezing profit margins and taking away jobs. In 2013, on a visit to Michigan in the US, I saw a large number of signboards lining the sides of major roads proclaiming: 'Back off Wal-Mart. Not our towns!!' One photograph which I took is reproduced below.

We must consider this reality – that the collective profit earned from the consumption behaviour of a combined population of 135 crore people could be drained out of India, if multinational retailers capture major market share – a reality that is imminent in the next few years. This will wipe out small mom-and-pop stores, the small-scale traders, and create massive unemployment. Large-scale retailers operate on a profit-per-employee model, and this, coupled with increased automation, would lead to even more shedding of jobs, and the accumulation of profits and revenues in the hands of few corporations is likely. Last year, during one of my trips to the United States, I went to the 'Amazon go' store at Union Square in San Francisco. The store is completely automated. I downloaded the Amazon app on my mobile, scanned it at the entrance, and I was in through an automated entry. Whatever I picked up and walked out with, was billed to my credit card, and there was no need of manual billing or going to the cashier. This was something we used to think as a figment of imagination and far-fetched, when I led a retail chain as a Chief Operating Officer about two decades ago, and now, it is a retail model being tried by the likes of Amazon (Gupta R.P., Opinion, 2019), and soon, it will be a model for other big box retailers. Once it succeeds and scales up, the day is not far when it will be in India.

Jack Ma, said this to a Walmart Executive during an interview in 2015.

"I said we will make a bet: In ten years we will be bigger than Walmart, on sales.

If you want 10,000 new customers, you have to build a new warehouse and this and that. For me ?......two servers". (Cook, 2015)

And now, Walmart acquired the biggest Indian online retailer (Flipkart), and this should be an eye-opener for the future of retail in India.

For a large lower middle-class country like India, such FDI investments should not cheer us, but worry us, as what they are doing is not creating a 'Distributed Growth Model' – but an 'Accumulated Growth Model', where there will be automation, jobs will get squeezed, wealth will accumulate in the hands of a few, and moreover, the profits would get repatriated abroad. With COVID-19 having upset the economic scenario, we must take the following steps:

- Withdrawing FDI in retail may not be possible, but finding ways to limit its growth, is! If FDI in retail can be withdrawn, nothing like it.

- Eighty per cent of the products have to be sourced locally in districts where these large big-box retailers operate. Imports should only be allowed for products that cannot be produced in India. Overdependence on imports will dilute the 'Make in India' program and even render it ineffective.

- Provide institutional support, with hard and soft infrastructure, and in a planned manner – to small-scale traders and retailers so that they can easily upgrade and remain competitive. Set up the DEFA (District Employment & Entrepreneurship Facilitation Agency) & task it to give recommendations to retail establishments in any given area or city.

- Build Farmland Parks and operate FARM stores across the nation

- Even the existing domestic online retail space should have offline fulfilment centres, through existing retailers, so that employment in retail, and the segment itself, can grow. Innovation is totally missing in this segment, and we need to ensure it, across the value chain, to balance profits with jobs.

- The rights and interests of consumers must be defined and protected.

- National aspirations and political compulsions must be balanced. Any imbalance will compromise India's present and the future. We must move towards a 'Distributed-Growth Model' as a pre-requisite for ensuring sustainable growth, and creating a recession-proof economy. The current economic model of India is unsustainable. This is a model where the accumulation of growth happens in the hands of a few people (big investors and industrialists). Such growth will naturally lead to disparities between the rich and the poor.

A few datasets illustrate these disparities:

- 1% of the top 10% Indian population holds 77% of the total national wealth. 73% of the wealth generated in 2017 went to the richest 1%, while the 67 crore Indians who comprise the poorest half of the population saw only a 1% increase in their wealth.

- India produced 70 new millionaires every day.

- There are 119 billionaires in India, and the number of billionaires increased from 9 in 2000 to 101 in 2017 (OXFAM International, 2020).

- Wealth held by Indian billionaires increased ten times over a decade.

- Four out of ten billionaires have inherited their wealth.

- Total wealth of Indian billionaires is 15% of the GDP of India.

- 43% of the rent – thick billionaires accounted for 60% of total billionaire wealth in 2020 (OXFAM India, 2018).

Policies over the decades too have done no good to this country's population, and if the same policies continue, we will create more divide between the 'haves and have-nots'. They will increase the undue influence of the rich, and create large-scale unrest due to wealth accumulated in the hands of a few.

Given the fact that smaller nations are able to rake in more FDI due to the buying/spending power of their population, India needs to consider broad-basing and increasing the buying and spending capacity of its population. We need to achieve a Distributed Growth Model, else, the huge population base will remain mere statistic!

DEFA – District Employment and Entrepreneurship Facilitation Agency

'A planned city, without a planned economy, will become a ghost town of the future'

An unplanned local economy is bound to fail and create chaos. Most of the small businesses fail due to lack of institutional support and an understanding of how the market operates, what the consumption trends are, what the needs of the buying population are, and what their buying power is. There is no data available for any town in India. Imagine officials sitting in an air conditioned offices in Udhyog Bhawan (Ministry of MSME) and North Block (Ministry of Finance), and planning about the financial packages for these MSMEs, which operate in a different environment, and where these officials have never visited as ordinary folks, and/or rarely interacted with the beneficiaries. Hence, these people do not know the ground reality, but still, they claim that the financial package will bring back the growth to normal? It is time to think differently.

Every district should have a *DEFA*, which will act like a consultancy and funding agency for starting and promoting a business, based on the viability study of the particular business, taking into account various factors. It will access the markets, do the viability studies, help in funding and setting up of the business, and also in the marketing of the business. It would be a business facilitation agency. So, if an entrepreneur with a corpus of Rupees ten lakhs approaches DEFA for suggestion of a viable business, not only DEFA will guide him about the business, but it will also help in marketing of the business through the *DREAM project* (which is detailed ahead). The DEFA should be set up by the Ministry of MSME in each district, with extension offices in Farmland Parks (FEZ) in the district. This organization can be a partnership between the Ministry of MSME and local business schools, and other professionals, who can be hired from time to time, or, as and when needed. The role of the DEFA should be three-fold—to provide guidance to Entrepreneurs and MSMEs, and in the longer term, to boost employment, and the GDP per capita in the district, through the *DREAM* project.

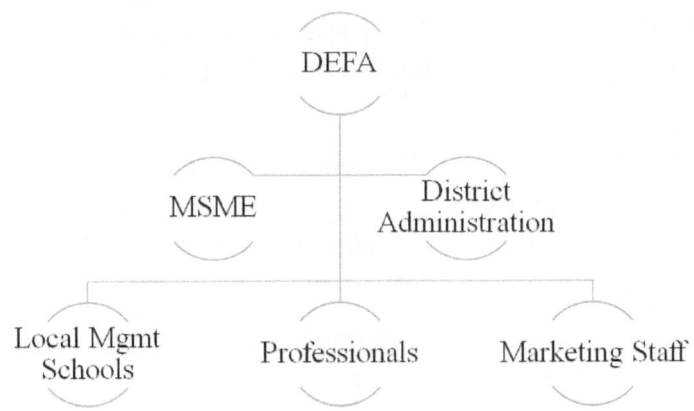

DEFA will;

- Set the vision for the district under its jurisdiction (GDP, Business, Jobs, and the needed infrastructure).

- Conduct research on business opportunities and their viability. Conduct market analysis studies, study and project the needs of the local population, the consumption pattern and per capita consumption, the consumer behavior, and define the parameters for the viability of a particular business in an area or locality, based on the needs of the local population, and the potential for exports.

- Identify clusters in every district for production units, and their needs in terms of machinery and manpower.

- Impart training for businesses that are based on local needs. Also, based on its analysis, DREAM project under the DEFA should provide marketing support to the local businesses.

- Create internship and 'earn while you learn' programs, and find appropriate opportunities for the professional engagement of senior citizens, based on their skills and fitness levels.

- Develop and implement quality assurance for products and services.

- Become a nodal point for the disbursement of government loans and grants, based on the viability of businesses.

- The permit system of starting a business should be done away with, and the DEFA should be the entity which decides which businesses can operate, based on the viability studies.

- Impart training and skill-development exercises to cater to local business needs.

- Identify and develop quality management systems, and ensure their deployment.

- Business units and entrepreneurs should be registered with the DEFA under the, 'One India, Single Window—One Business, One Registration' principle.

- Institute a district-level ranking of; Ease of doing business across the nation & the Livability index: All cities must be rated by its citizens on safety, access, connectivity, public amenities, taxes, health, education, environment, entertainment, employment, entrepreneurship, and the responsiveness of the administration and the public representatives. This will lead to a healthy competition for cities to become more citizen & business friendly.

From the government's perspective, there is an important reason to set up DEFA – the government is a default stakeholder and has between 26 to 43 percent stake in every company, as the government takes taxes on the income of the companies at an effective tax rate of 26%–43.68% (PWC, 2019). Moreover, without any investment, the government has only the upside (profits in business), and no downside (no liability towards losses). So, as a responsible stakeholder, government has all the reason to set up DEFA to ensure not just ease of doing business, but also to act as a facilitator for success of the business enterprise, so that it continues to enjoy the income from its stake (taxes it collects) in the venture. It is important for all the government departments that, interface with a business/entrepreneur takes place, to ensure ease of doing business and to facilitate the success of the business enterprise, as that is the primary deliverable of the government's *'shareholder for profit'* role (because of the taxes it collects). So, setting up of the DEFA becomes a natural obligation on the part of the government.

Most small businesses are set up with loans taken from moneylenders or banks, or with the funds raised by selling property or valuables. Should the business fail, whether because of a lack of knowledge of operating conditions, or other reasons; the entrepreneur and, in collateral damage, his family will suffer. To illustrate: On the Panvel–Matheran road in the outskirts of the Panvel area in Navi Mumbai, there is a stretch of five kilometres, which is sparsely populated. Four 'supermarkets' were already running here and a fifth 'supermarket' was coming up in 2018 when I wrote the book, 'Your Vote is Not Enough'. This was despite the presence of an umpteen number of road-side grocers. It is sure that the road-side grocers will have to close down because of competition from these 'supermarkets' and, eventually, even these 'supermarkets' will have to shut down due to competition amongst themselves, or because of them losing to some big-ticket retailer setting up shop in the area. These closures will hit the local economy hard and cause huge losses, not only to those who invested in the business, but also those whom they employed. As I write this book on economy, two out of the five have already shut down, and the third one whom I visited two months ago, had renamed his super-market on the name of a religious Guru. When

I asked him the reason for this name change, the owner responded, 'Sir, now that I have renamed it in the name of my religious guru, it will do well!'. Means that, this super market is also in doldrums. Due to closure post COVID-19, I am not sure if rest of the two will be there for the long run?

DEFA can be made self-sustainable by charging a small fee for its syndicate reports and studies, and for conducting customized market research as assessment and business feasibility studies for an entrepreneur. For women entrepreneurs, it can discount its services by 50 per cent Also, it can charge 0.5% for the loans disbursed under various government schemes.

DEFA is a must have for every districts. It is needless to mention that for the 640 districts in India, it will increase the available employment by at least 100 times, and contribute in making many more successful entrepreneurs. The DEFA should look comprehensively at all sectors, including agriculture and small retail stores. It should also forecast the manpower needed in the district, such as; barbers, cobblers, teachers, farmers, daily labourers, plumbers, carpenters, cooks, nannies, drivers, and security guards, among others. Also, for all funds related to the entrepreneurship schemes of the state and the central government, the DEFA should be the nodal agency for disbursement, and this agency can charge 0.5 per cent of the fund disbursed as its service fee for disbursal and for providing viability reports, guidance and ongoing business consultancy.

The DEFA should serve as an aggregator for making group purchases on behalf of its entrepreneurs to provide them a platform for collective bargaining in the purchase of raw materials. This is where the smaller logistics firms under DEFA, aggregators in villages, and small production factories in towns, will create a 'Distributed Growth Model' for India. Of all the government tenders for purchases and contracts, 60 per cent should be reserved for domestic bidders, and 25 per cent for Start-ups category. The remaining 15 per cent can be open tenders for global bidders, in the absence of which, orders may be awarded to domestic bidders and start-ups.

It is hoped that this organization (DEFA) will change the entire landscape of the self-employed, the professionals, the retail sector with its small scale enterprises, and small-scale industry. It will be the biggest contributor to establishing viable and profitable businesses and creating mass employment opportunities.

All this will not only make Indian economy resilient, but also provide employment and entrepreneurship opportunity, and mapping facilities across the country. If this project is implemented successfully as envisioned, we can create an *E-map—an Employment and Entrepreneurship map*—for every Indian town and village in the next three years. We could easily identify the kind of workforce and training we need for India, and address, to a large extent, the unemployment and business failure rate in the country.

To sum up: The current economic growth model of India is ad hoc and lopsided. Hence, we need to define a clear path for transitioning to the new economic model, which should be about 'Distributed Growth'. This new model is based on us achieving multiple targets: ensuring the self-sufficiency of districts; creating wealth for, and with, the lower and middle classes, rather than a few big business houses and MNCs; a drastic increase in public goods—in education, health and infrastructure; ensuring the availability of capital; removing bureaucratic legacies and red tape; and most importantly, reducing taxes— the government must understand that reducing taxes puts more money in the hands of citizens and this, consequently, will increase their buying power and boost revenue. The DEFA, the VKAP and the E-MAP will be important tools in ensuring sustainable economic development.

DREAM (District Retail & Employment Analysis and Marketing)

If one has money, or can arrange for it through a loan, the business can be started. But, the challenge starts when you are into the business – from getting the first customer, to increasing the customer base and retaining them, while understanding and managing the intricacies of stocking, merchandising, and supply chain management; balancing the human resources and profitability. This is where the dream project steps in – to help prepare entrepreneurs for these challenges.

DREAM will assist the beneficiaries of DEFA with regards to handholding for marketing support, and outreach to consumers through online and onsite campaigns, and in boosting the business growth and profitability. DREAM will also be the training ground of the management schools for testing the skills of their students, and honing them through practical exposure.

CENTER - Community Enterprise Township & Enclave for Residents

Given the migration of workers back to their villages and towns, it is time to consider setting up CENTER – A complete township with provision for non-emission enterprises (businesses which have zero emission), with Transit homes and Hostels for migrants with families, in towns where migrants come from other states like, major districts in Maharashtra, Punjab, Haryana, Kolkata, Karnataka, and different zones in Delhi etc. Also, it might be a good strategy to support the industries and factories in other towns and states by constructing Worker's Townships. When the investors (industrialists/business owners) see that the government has provided for workers residence and that there will be easy availability of labour, the factories are likely to come up in such towns with Worker's Townships.

The government must identify towns and clusters, and set up CENTERs, as large residential townships, equipped with; education facilities for the worker's children, healthcare facilities, banking, part time self-employment opportunities for other members of the family, along with skills development centers, stores run by migrant families, setting up of Self Help Groups (SHGs), setting up of transport facilities through proper public transport (eco-friendly bus service) – connecting to the places of work, etc. Also, these complexes could house business which do not have emissions (like, setting up weaving mills or Khadi centers), so that the complex is self-sufficient, and the produce can be linked up for online retail or exports from such centers. This will not only lead to better quality of life of workers, but also lead to availability of workers for local needs and upward mobility of workers in terms of their upskilling – to earn more and contribute more to the buying power of the economy. Finally, it will create local and self-sustaining economies.

VKAP - Vishwakarma Program

I ideated this program when I was called by the Union Minister for Labour and Employment in 2018, to address the Labour Ministers and officials from various states. It was on 18th April 2018 that I made a presentation about this program to various state level leaders about creating a Vishwakarma app (VKAP), to address the issue of – Identity, Productivity & Security, of about five crore Building and Other Construction Workers (BOCW).

Vishwakarma Program (VKAP)

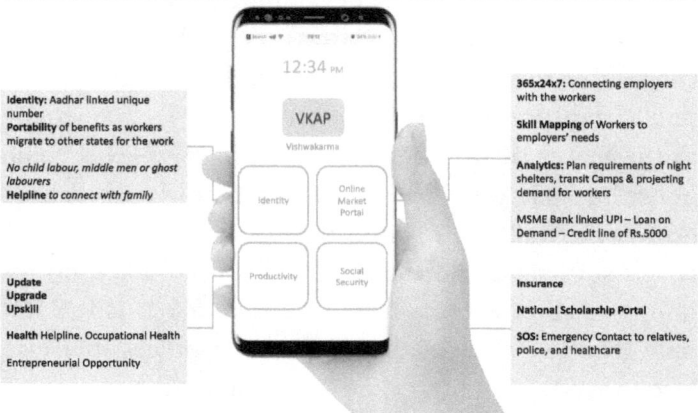

Identity: Aadhar linked unique number
Portability of benefits as workers migrate to other states for the work

No child labour, middle men or ghost labourers
Helpline *to connect with family*

Update
Upgrade
Upskill

Health Helpline. Occupational Health

Entrepreneurial Opportunity

365x24x7: Connecting employers with the workers

Skill Mapping of Workers to employers' needs

Analytics: Plan requirements of night shelters, transit Camps & projecting demand for workers

MSME Bank linked UPI – Loan on Demand – Credit line of Rs.5000

Insurance

National Scholarship Portal

SOS: Emergency Contact to relatives, police, and healthcare

We should build this app as a part of the *National Vishwakarma Program for Labour, Employment and Training*, and extend it to the entire informal workforce which is estimated to be between 85–93% of the total workforce in India (Mohanty, 2019). According to the Ministry of Labour and Employment, Government of India, *"As per survey carried out by the National Sample Survey Organisation in the year 2011–12, the total employment in both organized and unorganised sector in the country was of the order of 47 crores. Out of this, about 8 crores were in the organized sector and the balance of 39 crores in the unorganized sector. The workers in the unorganized sector constitute more than 90 percent of the total employment in the country. A large number of unorganized workers are home based and are engaged in occupations such as beedi rolling, agarbatti making, papad making, tailoring, and embroidery work"* (Ministry of Labour & Employment, Government of India, 2020).

It can be safely assumed that the number of workers in unorganized sectors may be more than the government's estimate of 40 crore, and they are not only unorganized, but also facing a lot of hardships when it comes to finding the right work, or even getting their due share in terms of remuneration or benefits of the government schemes. It is a common sight to see manual labours standing in sun & rain, waiting for someone to pick them up for the job, and most of the times, they may be in the wrong place and keep standing in adverse weather conditions, without getting a job despite demand, as the demand is in another area. VKAP should list all labourers across India including; house helps, security personnel, building and other construction workers, plumbers, carpenters, painters, electricians, sales assistants, etc. (with details of their skills, and work experience – along with a verifiable unique id), across India, and a list of employers as well. So, a labourer in north Delhi need not stand in the sun or rain whole day when he or she is needed in Noida, and similarly a labourer in Chennai should not keep waiting without an assignment in OMR (Old Mahabalipuram Road) when there is a desperate need of his/her expertise in Mahabalipuram or Pulicat. Vishwakarma app can help map the availability based on the needs, and the potential employers can connect with the prospective employees through the app and block his diary for the period the employer needs that worker. The Vishwakarma app could also serve as a platform for e-payment of the daily wages and to avail the benefits for various schemes of the government like; health, education and scholarship for children, pension, and insurance benefits. Most importantly, based on the work done, the employee/labourer and the employers can be informed about the applicable laws and the occupational health issues with regards to the job.

VKAP should also determine the labour charges for various trades and activities for the unorganized labour according to each town class. This will help ensure a fair and informed payment based on recommended charges.

With smart phones getting cheaper and 4G data available, it makes sense to leverage technology for unorganized labourers and make their lives easier, and enhance their earnings. Vishwakarma app can also help these mostly uneducated labourers to know their rights, and help them in skill enhancement through online tutorials, etc. Also, Vishwakarma app could provide a link to the nearest available night shelters or the CENTER/Workers Township hostel registration system, to avail of the subsidized or free accommodation from the government. VKAP can also help keep a track of the number of daily wage jobs created, and the wages earned by the labourers, and to design welfare schemes for such people and their families, and prevent cheating by employers. It can ensure payment of the appropriate wages through e-payment, and address the problem of ghost labour, grievance redressal, and ease the migration of labour. Also, the migrant labourer families could connect to their native place through the app, by a video call. Migrant labour could benefit from ordering online through the labour cooperative stores especially created for their needs by the government, operated by the labour community (or link it to *GeM – W; Government eMarket Place for Workers*). High time we do it.

The biggest challenge we faced during the COVID crisis was with the migrant labour force which panicked and started packing for moving to their native places. This has been a contributor to mass protests and also mass movement, leading to defeat of the purpose of a lockdown and spread of the COVID-19. If VKAP was available, then the respective states, in coordination with the centre, could have sent messages to the labourers. Also, cash transfers could have been done, and even activation or recharging of their phones bills, besides taking care of their movement via the location tracking. This would have even helped the government to be informed and be well prepared. Also, through VKAP, the labourers could have taken 'migrant insurance' for such natural disasters or calamities which would entail a one-time payment (given the experience of recurrence of such calamities, PSU insurance companies should start such a policy).

Also, based on prior learning, work experience, and proficiency based on the rating one gets on the platform, people can be awarded professional educational qualifications. And if they need to add on a certain skill, they could do so through a *National Vishwakarma University for Skills Development and Professional Training (This could be a digital university through VKAP)*. Clearly, there is a possibility that a plumber, based on the years of experience and expertise, can become graduate or a post graduate in the field, based on specialised skill acquired.

Digital MSME Bank - Loan on Demand

A digital MSME bank may be integrated to the VKAP and could be a good platform to promote entrepreneurship through 'Micro Loans'. So, if I am a worker in a specific category, and my work experience, and my daily, weekly or monthly income is visible on the dash board, then I could be extended a pre-approved 'Micro Loan', which is available through the UPI payment gateway option on VKAP. The credit line becomes a loan when I use the money available to me as a pre-approved loan, to pay for the purchases I may require for my work. This can be repaid back in a day, week or a fortnight, or a few months, with a basic interest. Government has to keep this in mind that it is not the 'static money in the bank' which adds to the economy, it is the money which changes hands that leads to value creation every time it changes hands, and that leads to economic growth. For example, when a plumber starts to buy the material with the 'pre-approved loan' on the VKAP, and then bills it to the customer along with labour charges, the money has changed hands (created value) eight times, if not more. Let us see how:

- Money transfer from VKAP to plumber – Interest is earned by MSME bank (1).

- When the plumber purchases a tap from the hardware shop – Profit is earned by the hardware vendor – retailer (2).

- Profit is earned by manufacturer of the product (3).

- Profit is earned by the logistics companies which supplied the product to the wholesaler (4).

- Profit is earned by the wholesaler from where it reached the retailer (5).

- When the tap, along with the service fee, is charged by the plumber to the client (6).

- Plumber will spend the money earned on multiple things and it is safe to assume that it will be changing hands at least twice (7,8).

So, a simple loan of Rs. 500 can end up in a multiplier effect if you look at the entire material production and supply process. A product, which was brought from the hardware shop, on a 'micro loan' would lead to further earnings (value addition), and the cycle would have continued unabated. Moreover, this is digital cash, and must be encouraged to be transferred digitally. When the consumer finally transfers money to the plumber for his services, say Rs. 800 (Rs. 550 for the tap and 250 fitting charges), the VKAP shows on his loan of Rs. 500.00 + 1 rupee daily interest on one hand, and cash paid by the consumer – Rs. 800 against it. The plumber, having made Rs. 300 on this investment, may want to clear it through the app by pressing a button on the same day, or pay it in parts, with interest. Also, VKAP can be used for opening a savings account and do an instant saving. This will also increase the saving rate for the nation. So, the cost of loan disbursal or operating a saving account, to the government will not be much due to tech driven disbursal, deposit and repayment, and the government can keep a track of the value creation and money changing hands. Also, formally money moving into the system means better tax compliance. This is where our formal banking system does not cater, but the economic opportunity of unorganized workers in this segment (totalling over 40 crores as per government estimates), can help in growth of the economy. So, the idea of a Digital MSME bank is specifically meant for providing loans from as low as Rs. 50 without any paperwork, to as high as an MSME needs, based on predefined criteria, or based on tax filings. No one should have to visit a bank, or an office, or feel shy of taking a Micro Loan. For those who doubt that loans disbursed to poor don't come back, have a lesson to learn from the micro finance experience at Grameen in Bangladesh that, 'Poor always pay back' (Dowla & Barua, 2006). There will be some defaults, but when people realise that without repayment, there is no additional loan and it is aadhaar linked, chances of default will be less. SIDBI or the MSME loans from Nationalised Bank would not work in such an environment, and the Government must initiate a Digital MSME bank for the same.

VKAP could be a major contributor to the 'Distributed Growth Model'. Vishwakarma app can be applied to every daily wage labourer, across sectors.

Integration of programs

As mentioned earlier, we must also work towards creating a government app called an *E-MAP* (Employment and Entrepreneur MAP), linked with the DEFA at the backend, to enlist all the daily wage earners, self-help group members, BOCWs (Building and Other Construction Workers), entrepreneurs, and MSMEs – on a national platform, and this will help in creating a platform to ensure that people are able to search for gainful employment. Also, those who wish to take financial assistance (Loan on Demand Scheme), and start their own business, could graduate from labourers, or wage earners – to business owners and job creators. We cannot even imagine the impact it will have in our entrepreneurship ecosystem and economy. So, someone who starts as a mason, carpenter or a plumber today, will end up being a hardware store owner tomorrow, or even become a serial entrepreneur running multiple businesses. We should be able to deliver such success stories through this system.

The DEFA, the VKAP and the E-MAP can become the biggest facilitators of the 'Distributed Growth Model', as the wealth generated through these businesses will remain localized in small towns and villages and with the lower and middle-income class. We can thus create a model where lower income class can move up the value chain to lower middle income and finally graduate to middle class, and some could become really successful businesspersons – HNIs and employment creators.

HEALTH Index

Despite implementing the most innovative programs and investing lakhs of crores of rupees, if we still measure the impact through the outdated GDP indicator, we would be groping in the dark. We need to come out with the country's *HEALTH Index (HEALTH-I)*, which captures comprehensive details of various performance parameters across; Health, Education, Environment, Economy, Longevity & Happiness. This index should be comprehensive enough to capture and convey the achievements or failures at the district level, aggregating to a regional or state level index, and finally into a national HEALTH Index. Without having a robust district level assessment, the national level index will hide regional disparities.

Digital Inclusion

We need a clear and comprehensive vision, and an implementation plan, for digital inclusion. We cannot become a digitally empowered society, despite having the best technical brains, if we keep using products made and designed in the US, that too, mostly by Indians. In the absence of home-grown solutions, we are overpaying the MNCs for achieving digital inclusion. This issue has to be addressed from the standpoints of all aspects related to digitization—software, hardware, network, hosting, and cybersecurity—and every aspect has to be led by Indians, with full knowledge that our digital horizons are expanding into Artificial Intelligence, Machine Learning, Quantum computing, Block chain, 3D Printing, Automation, and will go beyond what is comprehensible at present. In fact, what people call Artificial Intelligence is, I believe, the real intelligence, and it is here to stay.

These are a few concrete steps which India must take to ensure universal digital inclusion:

- India needs to move from being a body shop for the world in the digital field, to becoming a market and world leader. To achieve this end, we must aim at setting up small and large world-class institutes in every region which plug into larger institutes across the country. All these must produce the specialized human resources which are needed for the next one or two decades. The academia of these, as well as that of other institutes, should follow a 'revolving door' policy of spending time in the industry via sabbatical or other schemes. This will change the outlook – of academics, as well as that of those working in the industry, and make them aware of each other's culture and needs, and foster a more cohesive collaboration between the academia and the industry.

- We need to set up asset-light digital universities (Gupta R.P., Your Degree is Not Enough – Education for GenNext, p. 122).

- Indians cannot remain the best employees in the technical domain. We must become the best employers and entrepreneurs. It is Indian companies which should take the lead in providing solutions in the social-media and networking domains, in automation, as well as in cyber security and cyber warfare.

- Digital products and solutions are required for our entire population, and there is no reason why our expenditure in these areas should be remitted to the developed world. Be it the computer operating system, or conference solution, or games; we need to have Indian companies with leading products in every domain and sphere of working – right from the basic computing solutions to high end IOT products and services. We must build our own digital ecosystem. This gains even more urgency in the current scenario, where we are enthusiastically talking about building SMART cities. Now, we should talk of *SMART India*.

- Once we are ready with a roadmap, the government must mandate the use of technology in all spheres of governance and administration. By 2030, India must be a fully digital country where 100 per cent of the public services and interface happens digitally—safely and with cost-effectiveness.

- Elections can also be moved into the digital space, where electronic voting, linked to Aadhaar, will make it possible to enable everyone to vote from the comfort of their homes.

Real digital inclusion will happen only when we have a sound domestic ecosystem, with world class digital products, for which the world would be willing to pay a premium. We Indians can do it all by ourselves. All we need is a vision with a bold action plan, and with the government playing the role of a key enabler. Post COVID-19, we need to fast track the adoption of digital tools in keeping up with the framework of 'Sustainable Automation', which needs to be defined clearly and quickly.

(IAGF) India Assist Global Fund

India has lent a helping hand to nations in need – whether it was providing HCQ (Hydroxychloroquine), or Paracetamol, or PPE (Personal Protective Equipment) etc. – India does it under various circumstances, on humanitarian grounds. It is time that India sets an India Assist Global Fund (IAGF) which provides need based assistance to nations. There could be multiple other assistance, besides cash and supplies, like, assistance in consultancy and manpower. IAGF could be India's soft power diplomacy to show it cares for the world. Various Indian states could make specific contributions to this fund based on their local capabilities. But this should be only for international support and cooperation, for investing in the most pressing issues of the time.

Entrepreneurship

The ultimate result of right policies and good governance is a robust economy, and the end result of a robust economy is a job for every hand, which is the key for sustainable growth. If the country's citizens don't have purchasing power—which can only result from viable work opportunities—businesses cannot sustain themselves. Hence, it is imperative that either people have jobs or business to support their basic needs, or the government supports them by providing social security. Also, though getting investments for 'Make in India' is not difficult, unless we enhance the buying power of Indians, we will not be able to sustain 'Make in India'. In fact, consumers are the real financiers for the investments in any sector by any company, as investors need consumers to buy their products. So the government's focus on attracting large-scale investments across sectors could be a misguided step, without it *'creating consumers on a large scale, and not just large scale enterprises!'*

Given the protectionist policies being practised by nations across the globe, it is the need of the hour for us to formulate a plan to absorb members of the workforce who will be ousted from protectionist economies. The day isn't far—some countries in the Middle East have already begun doing so, as has the US. Many countries in the developed world will follow suit post COVID-19, as countries look at resetting the supply chain and creating self-sufficient and inward looking economies.

I have dedicated major portion of my earlier book, 'Your Vote is Not Enough' on Job creation, so I am not mentioning those opportunities here, but certainly, the government must seriously consider DEFA, DREAM, VKAP, E-MAP, Digital MSME Bank, and REWARDS program to encourage entrepreneurship.

REWARD Program

Government can set up a fast-track entrepreneurial helpdesk (*REWARD – Resident Entrepreneur With Attractive And Replicable Demo*) online, with a dedicated portal www.reward.gov.in. When the idea is submitted on this portal with details like, the business idea, along with basic financials and the team, it should go to sectoral and professional experts roped in by the government to evaluate the idea and to either accept, give inputs for modification, or reject the submission. The government must provide one year complimentary space in its start-up campus along with the basic necessities needed for setting up of the start-up, for free, and IT hardware on nominal rental basis; another twelve months on fifty percent subsidy, and then the start-up can move out of the campus or stay at the commercial rates. Government must pick up a small percentage of sweat equity depending on the period of free or subsidized utilization of services, say 0.5 percent, for every month the start-up avails the free/subsidized utilization of the start-up campus, not exceeding two years, and post that, the Start-up has to pay at the market rates. The same experts who evaluated the proposal may join as expert advisors for this start-up on honorarium plus sweat equity basis (from the government's share). This equity can be liquidated in 3–5 years as per the investment board of the start-up campus. Any registered start-up in such a campus should not be requiring any further registration or compliance, unless it is into hazardous business or strictly regulated business, for a period of three years. Even if regulatory approvals are required, the start-up campus should procure the same within two weeks of application through a single window clearance program.

Start-up campus must be set up in every university and in every district by the central government, or in partnership with the state government, and should be handled by professionals. Every start-up campus should aim at becoming self-sustaining over six to seven year time, through exit from sweat equity and rentals from commercial lease. This way, the start-ups will get free or subsidized space in the initial phase and later, when they grow, they can stay put by paying rentals on market rates, or move on. But this initial help will be quite useful in building a robust start up ecosystem in India.

SAFER (Savings Assurance for Every Retiree)

India needs massive investments for its infrastructure, and given that sixty five percent of the population is below thirty-five years in age, we must initiate a *'SAFER'* scheme. Under this scheme, the tax payer would be eligible for 6.0% of the total taxes paid as annual pension post the age of sixty, and farmers can be given a higher percentage, say 6.5 or 7%. With incomes rising with India's growth story, this scheme would meet the triple objective of;

a) increasing the number of tax-payers,

b) increasing the amount paid as taxes, and,

c) income earned will enhance the coffers of the government.

Cost of Job Creation

We must factor in one important input needed to plan and invest for job creation – the 'cost of job creation' – an important economic factor which I have never come across in any deliberation on economy or national planning. The cost of job creation can be calculated by the investment one makes to create a job. If one were to compare the cost of job creation between large conglomerates and Micro, Small and Medium Enterprises (MSMEs), MSMEs will be much more efficient at job creation than large plants and industries. We need to understand the underlying fact that it is not just about creating enterprises, but an enterprise where the cost of job creation is low. This needs a careful analysis for each sector and every segment of the industry. If we want quality jobs, we will have to work on this formula for 'cost of job creation'. For example:

- A restaurant in a middle-class town costs about Rs. 20 lakhs to set up in a rented location, and it creates jobs for six people, so the cost of job creation is Rs. 3.3 lakhs.

- In a town like Aligarh, setting up a branded gift shop would cost about Rs. 45 lakhs (Rs. 15 lakhs for the interior and Rs. 30 lakhs for stocks), and it creates employment for six people, so the cost of job creation is Rs. 7,50,000 per job. A showroom for watches costs about Rs. 1.50 crore to set up, and creates employment for six people, so the cost of job creation is Rs. 25,00,000.

- In a non-metro town, a shop that sells flower bouquets costs about Rs. 10 lakhs and generates employment for three people, so the cost of job creation is Rs. 3.3 lakhs.

- Setting up a retail pharmacy in a small-town would cost about Rs. 12 lakhs and provide employment to 4 people, so the cost of job creation is Rs. 3 lakhs.

- Setting up a typical village industry (small size), will cost about Rs. 5 lakhs, in addition to the cost of the land or rent. Such an industry will provide full-time employment to two people and the number of part-time workers may vary. Thus, the cost of job creation is Rs. 2.5 lakhs.

- Buying a vehicle so that it can be driven for an app-based ride-rental company, will require an investment of between Rs. 5 lakhs to Rs. 8 lakhs. If the vehicle is driven in two shifts, it can provide employment to two people, so cost of job creation will range from Rs. 2.5 lakhs to Rs. 4 lakhs.

- A typical handicraft industry in middle-class town costs about Rs. 60 lakhs to fund, and can create employment for twenty people. Thus, the cost of job creation is about Rs. 3 lakhs.

- One needs a minimum investment of about Rs. 30 lakhs to set up a petrol pump, which creates about ten jobs. So, the cost of job creation is about Rs. 3 lakhs.

- In rural area, it takes an investment of about Rs. 3 crores for starting 120 CSCs (Common Service Centres), which creates 120 entrepreneurs and 50 paid jobs – A total of 170 employees and entrepreneurs. So, the cost of job creation on a PPP model in rural India is about Rs. 1.76 lakhs.

- A sixty-bed cancer-care hospital in a tier-two town costs about Rs. 40 crore to set up and creates employment for about 300 people. So the cost of job creation is about Rs. 13.30 lakhs.

- A mobile manufacturing factory needs an investment of Rs. 800 crore (not factoring the land costs), and will create 5,000 jobs, so the cost of job creation is Rs. 16 lakhs. This does not include the cost of the land. (Mukherjee, 2018).

- A leading global manufacturer of mobile phones is investing Rs. 4915 crores and will create direct employment for 2,000 people (Khan A., 2018), which means the cost of job creation is about Rs. 2,45,75,000.

- A leading furniture giant announced that it will invest Rs. 5000 crore to create 4,000 direct jobs in Uttar Pradesh (The Indian Express, 2018). There the cost of job creation would be about Rs. 1.25 crore.

Thus, it is clear that, larger the enterprise, higher the cost of job creation. We will not be able to address this important issue of job creation, without factoring the cost associated with it. Also, here I have included only those businesses which will provide a minimum base income, which corresponds at least to that of the lower middle class. There are, of course, occupations and vocations, like that of street vendors, in which the cost of job creation is even lower.

If we target the creation of 1 crore to 1.2 crore jobs per year, with an average cost of 3 lakhs per job, we will need an investment of between Rs. 3 lakh crore and 3.6 lakh crore per year. This amount is definitely high considering that India's annual budget for 2019–20 was about Rs. 30.42 lakh crore and we had a fiscal deficit of Rs. 7.96 lakh crore (Ministry of Finance, Government of India, 2020, p. 1), in addition to the mounting debt, which has increased from Rs. 54.90 lakh crore to Rs. 82.03 lakh crore between June 2014 and September 2018 (IANS, 2019)—a jump of about 50 per cent in just four years. With lockdown due to COVID-19, the debt scenario is not going to get any better!

Taking into account that every percentage increase in GDP in India creates about 7,50,000 new jobs (World Bank, 2018), so, we need an annual GDP growth of 16 per cent to create the 1.2 crore jobs we need every year. But, at two to five per cent growth (which is the current growth rate and also the projected growth rate till 2022), we will create a maximum of 15 lakh to

37.5 lakh jobs a year and not the 1.2 crore jobs we need every year, and this means that, *the job deficit will add to the fiscal deficit. This twin deficit is going to create a serious social and economic challenge.*

Financing Growth

The problems in the economy did not start with COVID-19. We were already reeling under the prolonged slowdown since 2018, and I could foresee the same and wrote with data and facts in my book, 'Your Vote is Not Enough', way back in 2018. While I was reading the headlines of India looking at 8% growth, the numbers didn't convince me that we could reach even half of it in 2019 and finally, we saw our growth numbers tumbling down to sub-five percent growth. COVID-19 only exacerbated the already existing problem and compounded it. But after COVID-19, the business will not be usual. People who are waiting for lock down to be lifted, would have to struggle more to first accept the 'New Normal', and then, while businesses may be open and ready, their clients will take another quarter, if not more, to do business as usual. So, while entering lockdown was easy, getting out of lockdown is going to be pretty challenging.

Post COVID-19, the government will certainly provide financial stimulus for;

a) providing relief to people and businesses

b) investing in projects to prop up the GDP

But, the Indian Government's finances have already been stretched, and now, with tax collections falling, and fiscal deficits increasing to historic levels, we will have to think out of the box. It has to be a mix of incentives, investments and giveaways to build confidence in people, as a precondition to resurrect the economy.

Few things to consider:

1. We will have to take a massive hit in the ongoing financial year and we must be prepared for it.

2. We must set up the projects listed above: a) Vishwakarma b) CENTER – with Worker's Townships c) DEFA & FEZ (Farmland Park).

    These are not capital intensive (except for Worker's Townships – CENTER), but do we have another choice if we have to keep the businesses going, and divert the extra pressure due to migrants moving to rural areas, and also, at the same time, keep the investment coming from private sector in major towns to set up MSMEs?

3. Issue rupee denominated foreign bonds, "New India Bonds', which are backed by Sovereign guarantee, to raise equivalent of half a trillion dollars.

4. *'Diaspora bonds'* or *'Better India'* bonds for PIOs, NRIs to invest in. Those who invest upwards of 500,00 USD get dual citizenship. We must start dual citizenship.

5. *'New India Fund'* with tax-free donations must be initiated

6. Broaden the tax base before raising taxes – Launching of the *'Tax payer's pension scheme' (SAFER)*.

7. List PSUs in the stock market to raise capital, and divest if not of strategic value to the country.

8. Issue tax free annual interest payment bonds with ten, fifteen, and twenty-year maturity period, with the interest payable annually.

9. Given that we have about 10–12 lakh shipments per day from online retail giants, though the total transactions of 1.5 million is small, but could add up to raising about Rs. 55 crore/year if the government sought 1 Rupee donation per online transaction for the 'New India Fund'. This is a significant amount to be invested back in DEFA and associated projects.

10. Use the wealth stashed in religious trusts, except for the funds needed for the upkeep of the institutions. Though it sounds harsh, but idle money lying in such trusts is of no use at such times, and must be deployed for nation's development.

11. Take back fifty percent of the RBI reserves.

12. Lastly, print money.

Certainly, it would be out of place to assume that the Government will be able to achieve the budget numbers of revenue receipts of Rs. 20.20 lakh crores or capital receipts of Rs. 10.21 lakh crores, so, of the budgeted total receipts of Rs. 30.42 lakh crore (Ministry of Finance, Government of India, 2020), the shortfall will be at least 20 percent. And on the total expenditure of Rs. 30.42 lakh crore, could be 20% more – amounting to total of Rs. twelve lakh crore, and this is just back of the envelope calculations. The actual numbers may go much higher if the economy is not arrested from spiralling downwards. But certainly, we are looking at a fiscal deficit in excess of Rs. 12 lakh crore if we wish to invest decently to rekindle the economy and move towards a double digit growth. So, clearly, we will have to raise at least an equivalent of half a trillion dollars and invest in projects, which will catalyse further investments from the private sector. Also, we will have to shelve capital intensive projects which do not match with our national priorities in the post COVID-19 scenario, and revisit them in 2025.

Population Decimates Growth

The government of the day will have to ensure that population growth, economic growth, tax collection, income distribution and social security programs are in sync with the dependency ratio—a measure showing the number of dependents, aged between zero and 14, as well as those over the age of 65, to the total population segment aged between 15 and 64—and mapped to resources. We need to factor the dependency ratio in all our calculations, else we will find it hard to take care of elders with increased longevity (Dikshit, 2018). Also, mapping resources with population projections will be important to set a time-bound target for population control and to achieve the desired population-replacement level (Replacement level is the amount of fertility needed to keep the population the same from generation to generation. It refers to the total fertility rate that will result in a stable population, without it increasing or decreasing) (Searchinger, et al., 2013). So, this leads us as a nation to think of a population control law, and a common civil code.

India Will Emerge Stronger

PM's Foresight is Assuring

Let us consider the importance of three programs which were mentioned in the election manifesto of BJP in 2014 (I was involved in the drafting of the same). From the post COVID-19 scenario standpoint, it is clear that the vision of Mr. Modi was futuristic as these programs came in to our relief in a big way to handle the current crisis.

Digital India

A program aimed at Jan Bhagidari with moving to eGovernance. Add to this JAM (Jan Dhan – Aadhaar and Mobile) and you understand how it has come in handy in instant cash transfers during the COVID-19. This now needs to move to the next level of implementation to fully digitize a citizen's experience of the Government, and the citizens should ideally not have to visit a government office, except for registration of marriage and property (which even could move online).

Ayushman Bharat

India finally adopted after four decades what it promised as a signatory to Alma Ata in 1978. Ayushman Bharat is a scheme which gave the 'Right to Health' to 550 million poor. In the times of COVID-19, with testing being made a part of Ayushman Bharat, it appears to have been a timely designed intervention for the poor and the needy. This program, along with the Health & Wellness Centres, has impacted India's healthcare delivery.

Employment and Entrepreneurship

The program was finally implemented as 'Start-up India'. With COVID-19 crisis, all of us have seen how this 'Start-up' community got together at a short notice and made a positive contribution, by developing solutions to the challenge.

When I look at the above three programs and the other schemes, I am convinced that the vision of the government was well ahead of time, and in a way prepared India to handle COVID-19 in a much better manner than any other nation across the world.

Bibliography and Suggested Readings

WTO. (2020, April 8). *Press Release*. Retrieved from WTO: https://www.wto.org/english/news_e/pres20_e/pr855_e.htm

Gopinath, G. (2020, April 14). *IMF BLOG*. Retrieved from IMF: https://blogs.imf.org/2020/04/14/the-great-lockdown-worst-economic-downturn-since-the-great-depression/

Maliszewska, M., Mattoo, A., & Mensbrugghe, D. (2020, April). *Policy Research Working Paper*. Retrieved from World Bank: http://documents.worldbank.org/curated/en/295991586526445673/pdf/The-Potential-Impact-of-COVID-19-on-GDP-and-Trade-A-Preliminary-Assessment.pdf

Adrian, T., & Natalucci, F. (2020, April 14). *IMF Blog*. Retrieved from IMF: https://blogs.imf.org/2020/04/14/covid-19-crisis-poses-threat-to-financial-stability/

OECD. (2020, March 26). *Tacking coronavirus (COVID-19) – Contributing to a global effort*. Retrieved from OECD: https://www.oecd.org/coronavirus/en/

ILO. (2020, April 7). *ILO Monitor*. Retrieved from ILO: https://www.ilo.org/wcmsp5/groups/public/---dgreports/---dcomm/documents/briefingnote/wcms_740877.pdf

Mishra, A. R. (2020, April 14). *Live Mint*. Retrieved from Mint: https://www.livemint.com/news/india/barclays-cuts-gdp-forecast-for-india-to-zero-for-2020–11586848023858.html

IBEF. (2020, January). *Agriculture and Allied Indutries*. Retrieved from IBEF:
https://www.ibef.org/industry/agriculture-india.aspx

Gupta, R. P. (2020). *Your Degree is Not Enough: Education for GenNext*. Chennai: Mc Graw Hill.

Gupta, R. P. (2019). *Your Vote is Not Enough – A Citizen's Charter to Make a Difference*. New Delhi: Speaking Tiger Publishing Private Ltd.

Population, L. (2020, April 20). *Projection of Population*. Retrieved from Live Population:
https://www.livepopulation.com/population-projections/india-2045.html

PTI. (2017, June 21). *Poltics and Nation*. Retrieved from The Economic Times:
https://economictimes.indiatimes.com/news/politics-and-nation/indias-population-to-surpass-that-of-chinas-around-2024-un/articleshow/59257232.cms?from=mdr

PTI. (2019, April 17). *Politics and Nation*. Retrieved from The Economic Times:
https://economictimes.indiatimes.com/news/politics-and-nation/share-of-population-over-age-of-60-in-india-projected-to-increase-to-20-in-2050-un/articleshow/68919318.cms?from=mdr

Government of India, Ministry of Road Transport & Highways. (2016). *Road Transport Year Book (2015–16)*. Ministry of Road Transport & Highways, Transport Research Wing. New Delhi: Government of India.

UNCTAD. (2019, November 5). *UNCTADSTAT*. Retrieved from UNCTAD:
https://unctadstat.unctad.org/CountryProfile/GeneralProfile/en-GB/004/index.html

Reserve Bank of India. (2020, January). *ATM & Card Statistics for January, 2020*. Retrieved from Reserve Bank of India: https://rbidocs.rbi.org.in/rdocs/ATM/PDFs/ ATMCS0120201B73EC6DB20C4C9898CE7580037654BD.PDF

Singh, H. (2019, May 1). The Rise of the new middle class: No political party can afford to take them for granted. *Financial Express*.

Meyer, C., & Birdsall, N. (2012). *New Estimate of India's Middle Class*. Center for Global Development.

Wong, Y. H. (n.d.). *From Middle India to the Middle Class of India: Inclusive Growth as a path to Success*. Mastercard Center for Inclusive Growth.

Krishnan, S., & Hatekar, N. (2017, June 3). Rise of the New Middle Class in India and Its Changing Structure. *Economic and Political Weekly, LII* (22), pp. 40–48.

UNCTAD. (2019, June 12). *Global FDI slides for third consecutive year*. Retrieved from UNCTAD: https://unctad.org/en/pages/newsdetails. aspx?OriginalVersionID=2118

UNCTAD. (2020, January 20). *FDI inflows in 2019*. Retrieved from UNCTAD: https://unctad.org/en/pages/newsdetails. aspx?OriginalVersionID=2274

Office of the Registrar General & Census Commissioner, India. (2001). *Census of India: Migration*. Retrieved from Census of India: https://censusindia.gov.in/Census_And_You/migrations.aspx

Ministry of Housing and Urban Poverty Alleviation. (2017). *Report of the Working Group on Migration*. New Delhi: Ministry of Housing and Urban Poverty Alleviation.

Mohanty, P. (2019, July 15). *Industry*. Retrieved from Business Today:
https://www.businesstoday.in/sectors/jobs/labour-law-reforms-no-one-knows-actual-size-india-informal-workforce-not-even-govt/story/364361.html

Ministry of Labour & Employment, Government of India. (2020). *Annual Report 2018–19*. New Delhi: Ministry of Labour & Employment, Government of India.

Upton, P. (2019, November 12). *ASEAN as Asia's New Manufacturing Hub: Too Good to be True ?* Retrieved from ASEAN Briefing:
https://www.aseanbriefing.com/news/asean-asias-new-manufacturing-hub/

CENSUS 2011. (n.d.). *District Census 2011*. Retrieved from Census2011:
https://www.census2011.co.in/district.php

OXFAM International. (2020). *India: extreme inequality in numbers*. Retrieved from OXFAM International:
https://www.oxfam.org/en/india-extreme-inequality-numbers

Thacker, H. (2020, February 19). *Growth of Organic Farming in the World*. Retrieved from The CSR Journal:
https://thecsrjournal.in/growth-of-organic-farming-in-the-world/

Cernansky, R. (2018, February 20). *Environment I Future of Food*. Retrieved from National Geographich:
https://www.nationalgeographic.com/environment/future-of-food/organic-farming-crops-consumers/

PTI. (2019, November 30). *Agriculture*. Retrieved from The Economic Times:
https://economictimes.indiatimes.com/news/economy/agriculture/fertiliser-subsidy-arrear-at-rs-33691-crore-may-touch-rs-60k-cr-by-march-fai/articleshow/72309498.cms?from=mdr

Reisinger, D. (2019, January 10). *Briefing. Artificial Intelligence.* Retrieved from Fortune: https://fortune.com/2019/01/10/automation-replace-jobs/

Chuah, L. L., Loayza, N. V., & Schmillen, A. D. (2018, August 16). *Research & Policy Briefs.* Retrieved from World Bank: http://documents.worldbank.org/curated/en/626651535636984152/pdf/129680-BRI-PUBLIC-The-Future-of-Work-final.pdf

World Bank. (2016, October 3). *Speeches & Transcripts.* Retrieved from The World Bank: https://www.worldbank.org/en/news/speech/2016/10/03/speech-by-world-bank-president-jim-yong-kim-the-world-bank-groups-mission-to-end-extreme-poverty

Oxfam India. (n.d.). *Press Release Oxfam India.* Retrieved November 18, 2018, from Oxfam India: https://www.oxfamindia.org/press-release/6229

Income Tax Department, Government of India. (2018, December 20). *Tax Rates.* Retrieved from Income Tax: https://www.incometaxindia.gov.in/_layouts/15/dit/mobile/viewer.aspx?path=https://www.incometaxindia.gov.in/charts%20%20tables/tax%20rates.htm&k=&IsDlg=0

Dikshit, A. (2018, October 3). *Wealth I Plan I The Economic Times.* Retrieved from The Economic Times: https://economictimes.indiatimes.com/wealth/plan/old-age-dependency-ratio-getting-worse-in-india-underlining-need-to-save-for-retirement/articleshow/66049594.cms

Searchinger, T., Hanson, C., Waite, R., Lipinski, B., Leeson, G., & Harper, S. (2013, August). *Publications I World Resources Institute.* Retrieved from World Resources Institute: https://www.wri.org/publication/achieving-replacement-level-fertility

Manyika, J., Chui, M., Miremadi, M., Bughin, J., George, K., Willmot, P., & Dewhurst, M. (2017). *A FUTURE THAT WORKS: AUTOMATION, EMPLOMENT AND PRODUCTIVITY*. McKinsey & Co, MCKINSEY GLOBAL INSTITUTE. MCKINSEY & CO.

Shah, R. (2018, October 31). *Auto I Car News I Financial Express*. Retrieved from Financial Express: https://www.financialexpress.com/auto/car-news/finally-tata-harrier-full-images-out-heres-how-the-harrier-looks-like/1366696/

World Bank. (2016, October 03). *Who We Are*. Retrieved November 20, 2018, from World Bank: http://www.worldbank.org/en/news/speech/2016/10/03/speech-by-world-bank-president-jim-yong-kim-the-world-bank-groups-mission-to-end-extreme-poverty

World Bank. (2018). *Jobless Growth*. Washington: World Bank.

Mukherjee, W. (2018, November 29). Vivo plans to invest over Rs. 4,000 crore in India. *The Economic Times,* pp. https://economictimes.indiatimes.com/tech/hardware/vivo-plans-to-invest-over-rs-4000-crore-in-india/articleshow/66871796.cms.

Khan, A. (2018, July 9). Samsung opens world's largest phone factory in India; to create 2,000 jobs. *The New Indian Express,* pp. http://www.newindianexpress.com/business/2018/jul/09/samsung-opens-worlds-largest-phone-factory-in-india-to-create-2000-jobs-1840695.html.

Suneja, K. (2019, September 5). *Indicators*. Retrieved from The Economic Times: https://economictimes.indiatimes.com/news/economy/indicators/fdi-inflows-up-28-percent-in-q1-to-16–3-bn/articleshow/70986011.cms

IBEF. (2020, March). *FDI*. Retrieved from IBEF: https://www.ibef.org/economy/foreign-direct-investment. aspx

Fisher, D., & Mohan, A. (2020, April 21). *Facebook*. Retrieved from Facebook: https://about.fb.com/news/2020/04/facebook-invests-in-jio/

International Monetary Fund (IMF). (2019, April). *World Economic Outlook, April 2019*. Retrieved from International Monetary Fund (IMF): https://www.imf.org/external/pubs/ft/weo/2019/01/ weodata/weorept.aspx?pr.x=57&pr.y=10&sy=2019&ey= 2024&ssd=1&sort=country&ds=.&br= 1&c=534&s=NGDPDPC%2CPPPPC&grp=0&a=

Goyal, M. (2018, September 4). India's problem is to find jobs for 10–12 million new workers every year. *The Economic Times*.

World Bank. (2018, October). *Human Capital Index – India*. Retrieved November 20, 2018, from World Bank: http://databank.worldbank.org/data/download/hci/ HCI_2pager_IND.pdf

Malviya, S., & Chakravarty, C. (2018, November 05). Amazon goes shopping for Future Retail, to buy 9.5% stake. *The Economic Times*.

Gupta, S. (2017, September 23). Amazon buys 5% equity in Shoppers Stop for Rs179.25 crore. *Livemint*.

Business Today. (2018, September 19). Samara Capital-Amazon acquire Kumar Mangalam Birla's More supermarket chain. *Business Today*.

Countrymeters. (2018, November 21). *India Population*. Retrieved November 21, 2018, from Countrymeters.info: https://countrymeters.info/en/India

World Health Organization. (2018). *Air Pollution and Child Health: Prescribing clean air.* Geneva: World Health Organization.

ET Online. (2017, December 2). *ET – Economic Times.* Retrieved from Economic Times: https://economictimes.indiatimes.com/industry/banking/finance/banking/how-safe-are-your-deposits-if-your-bank-fails-read-about-the-bail-in-option/articleshow/61889538.cms

Express News Service. (2015, August 4). *Financial Express.* Retrieved November 21, 2018, from Land Bill: Govt to withdraw key changes: https://www.financialexpress.com/economy/land-bill-govt-to-withdraw-key-changes/113344/

Sirwalla, P. (2016, March 23). *Livemint.* Retrieved November 21, 2018, from Livemint: Home: Money: Full PF withdrawal before age of 58 difficult in most cases

ET Bureau. (2016, April 20). *The Economic Times.* Retrieved November 21, 2018, from The Economic Times: Wealth: https://economictimes.indiatimes.com/wealth/personal-finance-news/government-rolls-back-restrictions-on-withdrawal-of-provident-fund/articleshow/51896900.cms?utm_source=contentofinterest&utm_medium=text&utm_campaign=cppst

Hindustan Times. (2016, April 29). *HT Media Ltd.* Retrieved November 21, 2018, from Hindustan Times India: https://www.hindustantimes.com/india/roll-back-sarkar-five-decisions-that-modi-govt-went-back-on/story-B9SZeYAulFia38NpwqptEP.html

PTI. (2015, September 22). *The Economic Times – Tech.* Retrieved November 21, 2018, from The Economic Times: https://economictimes.indiatimes.com/tech/internet/no-restrictions-on-whatsapp-facebook-modi-government-withdraws-draft-encryption-policy/articleshow/49057581.cms

Livemint. (2014, December 18). Retrieved November 21, 2018, from Livemint:Home: Politics: https://www.livemint.com/ Politics/9DTeAuCaxomkOShIQHQXcK/Govt-withdraws-circular-on-Good-Governance-Day.html

The Hindu. (2012, May 7). *The Hindu – Businessline*. Retrieved November 21, 2018, from The Hindu – Businessline: https://www.thehindubusinessline.com/markets/gold/govt-rolls-back-excise-duty-on-gold-jewellery/article20430578.ece1

Hidustan Times. (2016, April 29). *Hindustan Times*. Retrieved November 21, 2018, from Hindustan Times – India: https://www.hindustantimes.com/india/roll-back-sarkar-five-decisions-that-modi-govt-went-back-on/story-B9SZeYAulFia38NpwqptEP.html

PTI. (2018, April 11). *Home: Nation: The New Indian Express*. Retrieved November 21, 2018, from The New Indian Express: http://www.newindianexpress.com/nation/2018/apr/11/ in-draft-rules-government-scraps-ban-on-sale-of-cattle-for-slaughter-1800126.html

Business Today: The India Today Group. (2018, July 19). Retrieved November 21, 2018, from The India Today Group: https://www.businesstoday.in/sectors/banks/modi-govt-plans-to-withdraw-frdi-bill-amid-public-backlash/ story/280420.html

India Today. (2018, April 3). *News/India: India Today*. Retrieved November 21, 2018, from Living Media India Ltd.: https://www.indiatoday.in/india/story/govt-withdraws-fake-news-order-on-pm-modi-directive-after-massive-outrage-1203488–2018–04–03

The Wire. (2018, August 3). *Government: The Wire*. Retrieved November 21, 2018, from The Wire: https://thewire.in/government/modi-govt-makes-a-u-turn-withdraws-proposal-to-create-social-media-hub

Borpuzari, P. (2018, February 2). *ET Rise – Policy & Trends: The Economic Times*. Retrieved November 21, 2018, from The Economic Times: https://economictimes.indiatimes.com/small-biz/policy-trends/government-defers-compulsory-e-way-bill-application-trial-to-continue/articleshow/62745402.cms?utm_source=contentofinterest&utm_medium=text&utm_campaign=cppst

Express News Service. (2016, December 31). *Business: The Indian Express*. Retrieved November 21, 2018, from The Indian Express: https://indianexpress.com/article/business/economy/demonetisation-50-days-74-notifications-central-government-narendra-modi-reserve-bank-of-india-rbi-rules-cash-crunch-ban-4452455/

Mondal, D. (2018, July 1). *Economy: Business Today*. Retrieved November 21, 2018, from Business Today: https://www.businesstoday.in/current/economy-politics/one-year-of-gst-tax-base-increase-to-complex-return-filing-system-find-out-the-successes-and-the-failures/story/279764.html

PIB, Govt. of India. (2018, June 27). *Press Information Bureau*. Retrieved November 21, 2018, from Ministry of HRD, Government of India: http://pib.nic.in/newsite/PrintRelease.aspx?relid=180247

My Gov. (2017, March 21). *Blogs: My Gov*. Retrieved November 21, 2018, from My Gov: https://blog.mygov.in/editorial/national-health-policy-2017-building-a-healthy-india/

My Gov. (n.d.). *Ministry of Women & Child Development: My Gov*. Retrieved November 21, 2018, from My Gov: https://secure.mygov.in/group-issue/inviting-comments-draft-national-policy-women-2016/

ET Bureau. (2018, April 3). *Policy: The Economic Times*. Retrieved November 21, 2018, from The Economic Times: https://economictimes.indiatimes.com/news/economy/policy/law-panels-suggestions-on-ibc-now-in-public-domain/articleshow/63602118.cms

PTI. (2015, May 22). *Poltics & Nation: The Economic Times*. Retrieved November 21, 2018, from The Economic Times: https://economictimes.indiatimes.com/news/politics-and-nation/real-estate-bill-in-public-domain-parliamentary-committee-seeks-feedback/articleshow/47382853.cms

Nanda, P. (2015, June 12). *Home – Politics: Livemint*. Retrieved from Livemint: https://www.livemint.com/Politics/jMq6hrM9Xa6CrcetrEtJ9N/Govt-plays-safe-puts-draft-IIM-bill-up-for-debate.html

ET Bureau. (2016, August 10). *News I Poltics & Nation I The Economic Times*. Retrieved from The Economic Times: https://economictimes.indiatimes.com/news/politics-and-nation/revamped-national-medical-commission-bill-put-in-public-domain-for-feedback/articleshow/53640097.cms

Ministry of Health & Family Welfare. (n.d.). *ME Division I Ministry of Health & Family Welfare*. Retrieved November 21, 2018, from Ministry of Health & Family Welfare: https://mohfw.gov.in/sites/default/files/Binder1_4.pdf

My Gov. (n.d.). *Department of Revenue: My Gov*. Retrieved November 21, 2018, from My Gov: https://www.secure.mygov.in/hi/group-issue/stakeholder-consultation-draft-model-goods-and-services-tax-law/?field_hashtags_tid=&sort_by=created&sort_order=DESC&page=0%2C24

Sinha, S. (2018, July 26). *The Business Line: The Hindu.* Retrieved November 21, 2018, from The Hindu: https://www.thehindubusinessline.com/economy/draft-gst-return-form-to-be-put-up-in-public-domain-by-monday/article24519131.ece

Ministry of Electronics & Information Technology. (2018, August 14). *Home I What's New I Feedback on Draft Personal Data Protection Bill.* Retrieved from Ministry of Electronics & Information Technology: http://meity.gov.in/content/feedback-draft-personal-data-protection-bill

Rao, P. (2014, December 2). *Adminstrator I Uploads I PRS Legislative.* Retrieved November 21, 2018, from PRS Legislative: http://www.prsindia.org/administrator/uploads/general/1417684398~~Parliament%20as%20a%20Law%20Making%20Body.pdf

Southwick, A. (2014, November 13). *Telegram.* Retrieved from Telegram: https://www.telegram.com/article/20141113/COLUMN21/311139991

Bates, M. (2016, September 15). *Guest Column I Daily Republic.* Retrieved from Daily Republic: https://www.dailyrepublic.com/all-dr-news/solano-news/local-features/local-lifestyle-columns/single-vote-can-make-a-difference/

The Library of Congress. (n.d.). *Jump Back in Time I The Library of Congress.* Retrieved November 21, 2018, from http://www.americaslibrary.gov/jb/recon/jb_recon_impeach_1.html

Maramkal, M. (2013, April 12). *India*. Retrieved October 29, 2018, from The Times of India: https://timesofindia.indiatimes.com/india/First-to-lose-elections-in-Karnataka-by-one-vote/articleshow/19515042.cms

D'Arpino, A. (2008, November 05). *Article I Mental Floss*. Retrieved from Mental Floss: http://mentalfloss.com/article/59873/10-elections-decided-one-vote-or-less

CBS News, Canada. (2014, April 8). *Elections I CBS Canada*. Retrieved from CBC News, Canada: https://www.cbc.ca/elections/quebecvotes2014/ridings/view/riding-104

TNN. (2008, July 22). *India I The Times of India*. Retrieved from The Times of India: https://timesofindia.indiatimes.com/india/BJPs-one-vote-defeat-in-1999-was-narrowest-in-history/articleshow/3261721.cms

Estepa, J. (2017, December 19). *Story I News I Politics I USA Today*. Retrieved from USA Today: https://www.usatoday.com/story/news/politics/onpolitics/2017/12/19/virginia-democrat-shelly-simonds-wins-race-one-vote-leading-house-delegates-tie/966485001/

Goswami, B. (2018, December 14). 6 panchayat candidates win by coin toss in Assam. *The Times of India*.

Dutta, P. K. (2018, December 13). Did BJP lose Madhya Pradesh to Nota and not Congress ? *India Today*.

Das, G. (2017, June 18). *Cover Story I Business Today*. Retrieved from Business Today: https://www.businesstoday.in/magazine/cover-story/going-going-gone/story/253260.html

Bureau, E. (2018, December 18). The Economic Times –
Indicators. *The Economic Times*, pp.
https://economictimes.indiatimes.com/news/economy/
indicators/niti-aayog-strategy-document-estimates-8-average-
gdp-growth-during-2018–23/articleshow/67160030.cms.

The Indian Express. (2018, December 20). IKEA signs MoU
with Uttar Pradesh govt, heads to Noida. *The Indian Express*
(https://indianexpress.com/article/business/companies/ikea-
signs-mou-with-uttar-pradesh-govt-heads-to-noida-5501273/).

PIB, Government of India. (2018, February 1). *Ministry of
Finance, Press Information Bureau, Government of India.*
Retrieved from PIB, Government of India:
http://pib.nic.in/newsite/PrintRelease.aspx?relid=176044

IANS. (2019, January 19). India's debt up 50% to Rs. 82 lakh
crore in Modi era. *The Economic Times.*

IBEF. (2018, October). *IBEF I Industry I Healthcare I Indian
Healthcare Industry Analysis.* Retrieved from IBEF:
https://www.ibef.org/industry/healthcare-presentation

Care Ratings. (2018, June 25). *Overview of the Indian Education
Industry I Care Ratings.* Retrieved from Care Ratings:
https://www.ibef.org/industry/healthcare-presentation

Ministry of Railways, Government of India. (2018, December 1).
Facts & Figures – Indian Railways 2016–2017. Retrieved from
Indian Railways:
http://www.indianrailways.gov.in/railwayboard/uploads/
directorate/stat_econ/IRSP_2016–17/Facts_Figure/Fact_
Figures%20English%202016–17.pdf

Seetharaman, G. (2017, November 26). *Industry I The Economic
Times.* Retrieved from The Economic Times:
https://economictimes.indiatimes.com/industry/
miscellaneous/heres-a-list-of-indias-geographical-indication-
tagged-products/geographical-indication-look-at-that/
slideshow/61805597.cms

Intellectual Property India. (2018, October 8). *Registered GIs/ Intellectual Property India.* Retrieved from Intellectual Property India:
http://www.ipindia.nic.in/registered-gls.htm

IBEF. (2018, October). *Brand India I Industry I Tourism & Hospitality in India.* Retrieved from IBEF:
https://www.ibef.org/industry/tourism-hospitality-india.aspx

PIB, Govt. of India. (2017, May 23). *Ministry of Electronics & IT, Government of India.* Retrieved from Press Information Bureau:
http://pib.nic.in/newsite/PrintRelease.aspx?relid=162046

IBEF. (2018, October). *Brand India I Industry I IT & ITeS Industry in India.* Retrieved from IBEF:
https://www.ibef.org/industry/information-technology-india.aspx

Raghuram, G. (2015, December 2). *An overview of the Trucking Sector in India: Signifance & Structure.* Retrieved from IIM-A:
https://web.iima.ac.in/assets/snippets/
workingpaperpdf/12319057932015–12–02.pdf

India Today. (2016, December 29). *News/Education Today/ Jobs and Career/A BFSI Career: Prospects and eseential skills.* Retrieved from India Today:
https://www.indiatoday.in/education-today/jobs-and-careers/
story/bfsi-career-prospects-360152–2016–12–29

Dovali, P. (2018, October 26). *Tech News/Gadgets Now.* Retrieved from Gadgets Now:
https://www.gadgetsnow.com/tech-news/mukesh-
ambani-has-good-news-for-mobiles-users-bad-news-
for-airtel-vodafone-idea/articleshow/66373741.
cms?utm_source=toiweb&utm_medium=referral&utm_
campaign=toiweb_hptopnews)

Indian Mirror. (2018, November 22). *IHome – Indian industries – Film Industry*. Retrieved from Indian Mirror: http://www.indianmirror.com/indian-industries/film.html

ET Retail. (2017, June 14). *ET Retail/Economic Times*. Retrieved from The Economic Times: https://retail.economictimes.indiatimes.com/news/industry/-indian-retail-industry-from-potential-to-performance/59141590

Government of India. (2018). *Educational Statistics at a Glance.* New Delhi: Ministry of HRD, Goverenment of India.

Bloomberg. (2018, November 1). *Bloomberg Daybreak: Middle East*. Retrieved from Bloomberg: https://www.bloomberg.com/news/videos/2018–10–31/yoga-pants-billion-dollar-industry-video

SENGUPTA, H. (2019, January 26). *Fortune India.* Retrieved from Fortune India: https://www.fortuneindia.com/polemicist/why-the-kumbh-mela-is-an-economic-blessing/102900

Khan, D. (2018, August 4). *Politcs and Nation/The Economic Times*. Retrieved from The Economic Times: https://economictimes.indiatimes.com/news/politics-and-nation/uidai-row-google-says-it-inadvertently-coded-the-number/articleshow/65264353.cms

GDPR EU. ORG. (n.d.). *FINES AND PENALTIES/ ADMINISTRATIVE FINES*. Retrieved from GDPR: https://www.gdpreu.org/compliance/fines-and-penalties/

Noorden, R. (2015, May 13). India by the numbers. *Nature News.* Retrieved from https://www.nature.com/news/india-by-the-numbers-1.17519

India Post. (2018, November 21). *About Us: India Post*. Retrieved from India Post: https://www.indiapost.gov.in/VAS/Pages/AboutUs/PostOfficeNetwork.aspx

ET Digital. (2018, September 5). *ET NOW – Home Business – Companies*. Retrieved December 2018, from ET NOW: https://www.timesnownews.com/business-economy/companies/article/direct-selling-companies-in-india-set-to-generate-nearly-2-crore-jobs-by-2025/278175

Gupta, R. P. (2015, January 17). *Can Make in India Learn Fom Make it in Germany*. Retrieved from Economy/Swarajya Magazine: https://swarajyamag.com/economy/make-in-bharat-is-the-need-of-the-hour

Reuters. (2018, June 6). *Reuters Business News*. Retrieved from Reuters: https://www.reuters.com/article/us-australia-economy-gdp-instantview/australian-economy-enters-27th-year-of-recession-free-growth-idUSKCN1J206K

The Economist. (2018, October 27). Australia's economy is still booming, but politics is a cause for concern. *The Economist* (Special Report), pp. https://www.economist.com/special-report/2018/10/27/australias-economy-is-still-booming-but-politics-is-a-cause-for-concern.

Swan, W. (2013, October 4). *AU Politics/The Guardian*. Retrieved from The Guardian: https://www.theguardian.com/commentisfree/2013/oct/04/australia-economy-labor

The Economist. (2018, October 27). What the world can learn from Australia. *The Economist* (Print Edition I Leaders), pp. https://www.economist.com/leaders/2018/10/27/what-the-world-can-learn-from-australia.

Gupta, R. P. (2016). *Healhcare Reforms in India ; Making up for the lost decades.* Delhi: Elsevier.

Registrar General & Census Commissioner, Govt. of India. (2018, November 13). *Age Structure And Marital Status.* Retrieved from Registrar General & Census Commissioner, Govt. of India: http://censusindia.gov.in/Census_And_You/age_structure_and_marital_status.aspx

World Health Organization. (2018, September). *World Health Organization – Health Topics: Gaming Disorder.* Retrieved from World Health Organization: https://www.who.int/features/qa/gaming-disorder/en/

World Health Organization. (2018, November 13). *World Health Organization: Regional Offfice for South – East Asia.* Retrieved from World Health Organization: http://www.searo.who.int/mediacentre/releases/2016/1631/en/

UNDP. (2018, November 13). *Sustainable Development Goals.* Retrieved from UNDP: http://www.undp.org/content/undp/en/home/sustainable-development-goals.html

Biography. (2017, December 1). *Biography.* Retrieved from Charles Darwin/Biography: https://www.biography.com/people/charles-darwin-9266433

Biography. (2017, April 27). *Gregor Mendel/Biography.* Retrieved from Biography: https://www.biography.com/people/gregor-mendel-39282

Biography. (2018, January 4). *Louis Pasteur/Biography.* Retrieved from Biography: https://www.biography.com/people/louis-pasteur-9434402

NobelPrize.org. (2018, November 22). *Albert Einstein – Biographical*. Retrieved from The Nobel Prize: https://www.nobelprize.org/prizes/physics/1921/einstein/biographical/

Strauss, V. (2016, February 11). *Answer Sheet – The Washington Post*. Retrieved from The Washington Post: https://www.washingtonpost.com/news/answer-sheet/wp/2016/02/11/was-albert-einstein-really-a-bad-student-who-failed-math/?noredirect=on&utm_term=.f1d916d97c36

Biography. (2017, August 1). *Isaac Newton – Biography*. Retrieved from Biography: https://www.biography.com/people/isaac-newton-9422656

Hawking, S. (2018). *BRIEF ANSWERS TO THE BIG QUESTIONS*. London, Londay, U.K.: John Murray (Publishers).

Biography. (2017, August 1). *Galileo – Biograpy*. Retrieved from Biography: https://www.biography.com/people/galileo-9305220

Biography. (2017, April 27). *Martin Twain – Biography*. Retrieved from Biography: https://www.biography.com/people/mark-twain-9512564

The Best Schools. (2018, November 20). *The Top 50 Economists from 1900 to the Present*. Retrieved from The Best Schools: https://thebestschools.org/features/top-economists-1900-to-present/

Ministry of Finance, Government of India. (2018, January). *Economic Survey 2017–18*. Retrieved from Ministry of Finance: http://mofapp.nic.in:8080/economicsurvey/pdf/119–130_Chapter_08_ENGLISH_Vol_01_2017–18.pdf

IBEF. (2017, June). *Brand India/Industry/Research and Development in India*. Retrieved from IBEF: https://www.ibef.org/industry/research-development-india.aspx

TNN. (2018, May 3). *World – The Times of India*. Retrieved from The Times of India: https://timesofindia.indiatimes.com/world/india-has-14-out-of-15-most-polluted-cities-in-the-world-/articleshow/63997961.cms

World Bank. (n.d.). *Data – World Bank Country and Lending Groups*. Retrieved November 22, 2018, from World Bank: https://datahelpdesk.worldbank.org/knowledgebase/articles/906519

The Indian Express. (2018, January 4). Govt says no proposal to review Most Favored Nation status to Pakistan. *The Indian Express*.

Press Trust of India. (2018, November 14). No plans to grant Most Favoured Nation status to India, says Pakistan government. *The Hindustan Times*.

Lok Sabha Secretariat. (2018, July 25). *Lok Sabha Committees*. Retrieved from Lok Sabha: http://164.100.47.193/lsscommittee/Estimates/16_Estimates_29.pdf

BBC. (2017, July 12). *BBC News Asia India*. Retrieved November 2018, from BBC: Indian mutiny: Remembering farmers who fought British rule

Rajawat, Y. (2018, October 4). *Opinion – DNA*. Retrieved from DNA India: https://www.dnaindia.com/india/report-dna-opinion-farmers-suffer-while-leaders-have-a-field-day-2671335

Nair, R. (2018, August 17). Over 50% agricultural households are facing indebtness: Nabard. *Mint, 12(197), New Delhi*. New Delhi, Delhi, India: HT Media.

Sirohi, N. (2018). *To double the farmer's income – A promise.* Delhi: Jebu Research Private Limited.

NationMaster. (2018, September 30). *Agriculture > Arable land > Hectares: Countries Compared.* Retrieved September 30, 2018, from NationMaster: http://www.nationmaster.com/country-info/stats/Agriculture/Arable-land/Hectares#2005

Roy, V. C. (2013, March 30). Punjab facing stagnancy in agriculture: State's Economic Survey. *Business Standard,* pp. https://www.business-standard.com/article/economy-policy/punjab-facing-stagnancy-in-agriculture-state-s-economic-survey-113033000131_1.html.

Peerzada, A. R. (2018, 5 16). *BBC News Business.* Retrieved from BBC: https://www.bbc.com/news/business-43962688

Khanday, Z. A., & Akram, M. (2012). Health Status of Marginalized Groups in India. *International Journal of Applied Sociology,* 60–70.

Sanghvi, D. (2018, November 6). *Money – Livemint.* Retrieved from Livemint: https://www.livemint.com/Money/Utjk0gDJvqynI8Ua3wiuZN/As-we-age-the-rising-demand-for-senior-care-will-make-sup.html

CII. (2018). *CII – Senior Care Industry Report India 2018.* Delhi: CII.

RESEARCH AND MARKETS. (n.d.). *The India 2018 Wealth Report.* Retrieved November 21, 2018, from RESEARCH AND MARKETS: https://www.researchandmarkets.com/reports/4580166/the-india-2018-wealth-report

Krishnan, S., & Hatekar, N. (2017, June 3). Special Articles – Economic & Political Weekly. *Economic & Political Weekly, 52*(22). Retrieved from Economic & Political Weekly: https://www.epw.in/journal/2017/22/special-articles/rise-new-middle-class-india-and-its-changing-structure.html

Reserve Bank of India. (2018, October). *ATM & Card statistics for August 2018*. Retrieved from Reserve Bank of India: https://rbidocs.rbi.org.in/rdocs/ATM/PDFs/ATMC0820187FB940DB7996455284154AEE2E84D43D.PDF

PIB, Ministry of Finance, Government of India. (2018, August 7). *Ministry of Finance, Government of India*. Retrieved from Press Information Bureau: http://pib.nic.in/newsite/PrintRelease.aspx?relid=181634

Ministry of Finance, Government of India. (2018, January). *Economic Survey 2017–18*. Retrieved from Economic Survey 2017–18: http://mofapp.nic.in:8080/economicsurvey/pdf/120–150_Chapter_08_Economic_Survey_2017–18.pdf

UNCTAD. (2018). *World Investment Report 2018*. Geneva: United Nations Pubications.

Kim, H. (2017, AUGUST 9). The Efffect of Consumption on Economic Growth in Asia. *Journal of Global Economics*.

The Economic Times. (2019, January 22). 'FDI Inflows: India at No. 10'. *The Economic Times*, p. https://epaper.timesgroup.com/Olive/ODN/TheEconomicTimes/shared/ShowArticle.aspx?doc=ETM%2F2019%2F01%2F22&entity=Ar02012&sk=8DBCC186&mode=image.

Gupta, R. P. (2019, January 29). 'Distributed Growth Model' Is The Need Of The Hour. Growth Alone Will Not Suffice. *Outlook*.

Gupta, R. P. (2018, 9 9). *Money*. Retrieved from Daily O:
    https://www.dailyo.in/business/wto-donald-trump-trade-
    wars-world-bank-agriculture-subsidies/story/1/26544.html

Times of India. (2018, July 25). *India – The Times of India*.
    Retrieved from The Times of India:
    https://timesofindia.indiatimes.com/india/parliament-passes-
    bill-to-punish-bribe-givers-along-with-takers-highlights/
    articleshow/65127834.cms

Mishra, D. (2018, November 5). *The Times of India*. Retrieved
    from The Times of India:
    https://epaper.timesgroup.com/Olive/ODN/TimesOfIndia/
    shared/ShowArticle.
    aspx?doc=TOIM%2F2018%2F11%2F05&entity=Ar02513&sk=
    E0356873&mode=text

UNESCO. (n.d.). *Diversity of Cultural Expressions – UNESCO*.
    Retrieved November 21, 2018, from UNESCO:
    https://en.unesco.org/creativity/convention

Ranade, A. (2018, April 4). *Opinion – Livemint*. Retrieved from
    Livemint:
    https://www.livemint.com/
    Opinion/7unVzUcfBJxbHHaiRpenmK/India-should-begin-
    discussing-the-delimitation-question.html

World Population Review. (n.d.). *World Population Review*.
    Retrieved November 21, 2018, from World Population Review:
    http://worldpopulationreview.com/countries/

FAO. (2020). *India at a Glance*. Retrieved from FAO:
    http://www.fao.org/india/fao-in-india/india-at-a-glance/en/

Ministry of Finance, Government of India. (2020). *Economic
    Survey 2019–20*. New Delhi: Ministry of Finance, Government
    of India.

IBEF. (2020, April 23). *Brand India – Industry – Agriculture in India: Information about Indian Agriculture & its importance.* Retrieved from IBEF: https://www.ibef.org/industry/agriculture-india.aspx

IBEF. (2020). *Telecommunications.* Delhi: IBEF.

Invest India. (2020). *Telecom.* Retrieved from Invest India: https://www.investindia.gov.in/sector/telecom

Sarkar, S. (2019, November 1). *Bloomberg Quint.* Retrieved from Bloomberg Quint: https://www.bloombergquint.com/markets/government-will-be-the-biggest-loser-if-a-telecom-operator-collapses

Naidu, K. (2019, August 30). *Home Business.* Retrieved from Business Insider India: https://www.businessinsider.in/mukesh-ambanis-telecom-war-escalates-telecom-industry-debt-to-3–9-lakh-crore/articleshow/70906000.cms

PTI. (2019, September 25). *Telecome News.* Retrieved from The Economic Times: https://economictimes.indiatimes.com/industry/telecom/telecom-news/telecom-sector-revenue-slips-7-per-cent-in-2018-trai/articleshow/71299512.cms?from=mdr

Gupta, R. P. (2019, July 11). *DNA.* Retrieved from Home I Analysis: https://www.dnaindia.com/analysis/column-what-s-the-hurry-to-import-5g-2770635

Gupta, R. P. (2019). *Your Vote is Not Enough – A Citizen's Charter to Making a Difference.* Delhi: Speaking Tiger Publishing Private Limited.

Gupta, R. P. (2015, January 17). Can Make In India Learn From Make It In Germany. *SWARAJYA.*

World Bank. (2020). *Data*. Retrieved from World Bank: https://datahelpdesk.worldbank.org/knowledgebase/articles/906519-world-bank-country-and-lending-groups

Gupta, R. P. (2018, January 29). *Opinion*. Retrieved from Outlook India: https://www.outlookindia.com/website/story/distributed-growth-model-is-the-need-of-the-hour-growth-alone-will-not-suffice/307505

Gupta, R. P. (2019, September 5). *Opinion*. Retrieved from Outlook India: https://www.outlookindia.com/website/story/india-news-opinion-automation-will-only-exacerbate-an-already-bad-situation-in-job-market-created-by-globalisation/337950

PWC. (2019, December 20). *India: Corporate – Taxes on corporate income*. Retrieved from PWC: https://taxsummaries.pwc.com/india/corporate/taxes-on-corporate-income

IBEF. (2020, March). *Foreign Institutional Investors*. Retrieved from IBEF: https://www.ibef.org/economy/foreign-institutional-investors.aspx

PIB. (2020, March 4). *Sector-Wise FDI Inflow*. Retrieved from PIB: https://pib.gov.in/newsite/PrintRelease.aspx?relid=199821

Xinhua. (2020, April 7). *XINHUANET*. Retrieved from Xinhua: http://www.xinhuanet.com/english/2020–04/07/c_138954840.htm

UNCTAD. (2019, November 5). *UNCTADSTAT*. Retrieved from UNCTAD: https://data.worldbank.org/country/india

Ministry of Finance, Government of India. (2020, February 1). *Budget at a Glance.* Retrieved from India Budget: https://www.indiabudget.gov.in/doc/Budget_at_Glance/bag1.pdf

Gupta, R. P. (n.d.). *Your Degree is Not Enough – Education for GenNext.* Chennai: Mc Graw Hill Education (India) Pvt. Ltd.

Gupta, R. P. (2019). *Your Vote is Not Enough – Citizens Charter for Making a Difference.* Delhi: Speaking Tiger Publishing Private Limited.

Ghose, D. (2020, April 27). *India.* Retrieved from The Indian Express: https://indianexpress.com/article/india/covid-fighting-infrastructure-isolation-beds-shortage-ventilators-icu-beds-6380747/

PTI. (2017, August 31). *LiveMint.* Retrieved from LiveMint: https://www.livemint.com/Politics/cEkjcsR2cLWoRqqB0lqgDM/290-children-died-at-Gorakhpur-BRD-Medical-College-this-Augu.html

Reuters. (2020, January 6). *India Today.* Retrieved from India Today: https://www.indiatoday.in/india/story/children-s-death-toll-rajasthan-kota-1634252–2020–01–06

WHO. (2020, April 27). *Coronavirus disease (COVID-2019) situation reports.* Retrieved from WHO: https://www.who.int/emergencies/diseases/novel-coronavirus-2019/situation-reports

Gupta, R. P. (2020, March 29). *Note from a Policy Maker.* Retrieved from Outlook India: https://www.outlookindia.com/website/story/opinion-what-india-could-have-done-to-better-handle-the-deadly-coronavirus/349649

PTI. (2020, April 26). *Policy*. Retrieved from The Economic Times:
https://economictimes.indiatimes.com/news/economy/
policy/funding-coronavirus-fight-tax-officers-suggest-
40-tax-on-super-rich-higher-levy-on-foreign-cos/
articleshow/75389146.cms?from=mdr

Tangel, A. (2020, April 27). *Business*. Retrieved from The Wall Street Journal:
https://www.wsj.com/articles/boeing-ceo-sees-slow-recovery-
for-global-aviation-11587999081

The Banking & Finance Post. (2020, April 27). *NEWS*. Retrieved from The Banking & Finance Post:
https://bfsi.eletsonline.com/nearly-half-of-indias-smes-
exhausted-their-funds-survey/

Didyala, A. (2020, April 28). *Hyderabad*. Retrieved from The Times of India:
https://timesofindia.indiatimes.com/city/hyderabad/
occupancy-dives-hospitals-in-city-reel-under-huge-losses/
articleshow/75416623.cms?utm_medium=referral&utm_
campaign=iOSapp&utm_source=email

UNCTAD. (2019). *World Investment Report 2019*. Geneva: UNCTAD.

Gupta, R. P. (2015, January 17). *Economy*. Retrieved from Swarajya Magazine:
https://swarajyamag.com/economy/make-in-bharat-is-the-
need-of-the-hour

Ministry of Finance, Government of India. (2020, February). *Union Budget*. Retrieved from India Budget:
https://www.indiabudget.gov.in/budgetglance.php

Express News Service. (2020, February 23). *Farmer suicides on the rise under Modi regime.* Retrieved from The New Indian Express:
https://www.newindianexpress.com/cities/thiruvananthapuram/2020/feb/23/farmer-suicides-on-the-rise-under-modi-regime-2107280.html

Gupta, R. P. (2019). *Your Vote is Not Enough – Citizen's Charter to Making a Difference.* Delhi: Speaking Tiger Publishing Private Limited.

United Nations. (2020). *Population.* Retrieved from United Nations:
https://www.un.org/en/sections/issues-depth/population/index.html

World Bank. (2019, July 1). *World Bank Blogs.* Retrieved from World Bank:
https://blogs.worldbank.org/opendata/new-country-classifications-income-level-2019–2020

Ministry of Health & Family Welfare, Government of India. (2020). *National Health Portal.* Retrieved from National Health Portal:
https://www.nhp.gov.in/nhpfiles/national_health_policy_2017.pdf

Shodhganga. (2020). *Electricity and Demand Projections.* Retrieved from Shodhganga:
https://shodhganga.inflibnet.ac.in/bitstream/10603/8179/10/10_chapter%2003.pdf

IBEF. (2020, February). *Indian Power Industry.* Retrieved from IBEF:
https://www.ibef.org/download/Power-February-2020.pdf

Dutta, S. (2019, August 2). *India Business*. Retrieved from The Times of India:
https://timesofindia.indiatimes.com/business/india-business/india-will-use-more-power-than-europe-us-by-2040-study/articleshow/70504132.cms

Gupta, R. P. (2020). *Your Degree is Not Enough – Education for GenNext*. Chennai: McGraw Hill Education (India) Pvt. Ltd.

OXFAM India. (2018). *India Inequity Report 2018 – Widening Gaps*. New Delhi: Oxfam India.

Dowla, A., & Barua, D. (2006). *The Poor Always Pay Back*. Bloomfield: Kumarian Press Inc.

Ministry of Finance, Government of India. (2020, February). *Union Budget 2020–21*. Retrieved April 2020, from Ministry of Finance, Government of India:
https://www.indiabudget.gov.in/doc/Budget_at_Glance/bag1.pdf

KPMG. (2020). *Potential Impact of COVID-19 on the Indian Economy*. KPMG.

Tarki, A., Levy, P., & Weiss, J. (2020). *Recession*. Massachusetts: Harvard Business School Publishing Corporation.

TNN. (2020, March 27). *The Times of India*. Retrieved from The Times of India:
https://timesofindia.indiatimes.com/india/day-2-of-lockdown-truckers-abandon-vehicles-delivery-boys-fret-about-safety/articleshow/74838109.cms

PIB, Government of India. (2019, July 12). *Self Help Groups*. Retrieved from PIB, Government of India:
https://pib.gov.in/newsite/PrintRelease.aspx?relid=191635

Cook, J. (2015, January 23). *Home > Tech*. Retrieved from
   Business Insider India:
   https://www.businessinsider.in/tech/jack-ma-heres-
   how-alibaba-will-become-bigger-than-walmart/
   articleshow/45993028.cms

Acknowledgements

COVID-19 taught us all some important lessons; set the right priorities, invest time judiciously, find the right resources, and move quickly.

The book would not have been in your hands in less than three weeks of my deciding to write had the following people not helped by accommodating my requests;

- Naveen Valsakumar, CEO of Notion Press, and his team, for committing to bring out the hard copies in ten days of submitting the manuscript. Also I wish to thank; Vishal Menon, Gabriela Caster, Abdul Rahman, Gokul Ramaraj, Subbhaiya Perumal at Notion Press,

- Dr. Rahul K. Garg, for quickly turning around the data into meaningful infographics

- Kopal Gupta for critically reviewing the book

- Reyansh Gupta (Happy) for allowing me to work, without bothering me, and serving me numerous cups of tea and coffee to keep me caffeinated

- Organizations whom I consult or advice, for letting me to skip a few conference calls due to tight timelines

Thank You ☺

The Power of One

One song can spark a moment,
One flower can wake the dream.

One tree can start a forest,
One bird can herald a spring.

One smile begins a friendship,
One handclasp lifts a soul.

One star can guide a ship at sea,
One word can frame the goal.

One vote can change a nation,
One sunbeam lights a room.

One candle wipes out darkness,
One laugh will conquer gloom.

One step must start each journey,
One word must start each prayer.

One hope will raise your spirits,
One touch can show you care.

One voice can speak with wisdom,
One heart can know what's true.

One life can make the difference,
You see, IT's UP TO YOU!
(Author Unknown)